DISMANTLING RACISM

The Continuing Challenge
to White America

Joseph Barndt

Augsburg   Minneapolis

DISMANTLING RACISM
The Continuing Challenge to White America

Scripture quotations unless otherwise noted are from the New Revised Standard Version of the Bible, copyright © 1989 by the Division of Christian Education of the National Council of Churches.

Cover design: Ned Skubic
Interior design: Carol Evans-Smith

Library of Congress Cataloging-in-Publication Data

Barndt, Joseph R.
    Dismantling racism : the continuing challenge to white America / Joseph Barndt.
        p. cm.
    Includes bibliographical references.
    ISBN 0-8066-2576-7 (alk. paper)
    1. Racism—United States.   2. Racism—Religious aspects—Christianity.
    3. Church and social problems—United States.   4. United States—Race relations.
    I. Title.
    E185.615.B339   1991
    305.8'00973—dc20   91-23449
                                                                                 CIP

The paper used in this publication meets the minimum requirements of American National Standard for Information Sciences—Permanence of Paper for Printed Library Materials, ANSI Z329.48-1984. ∞™

Manufactured in the U.S.A.   AF 9-2576

95   94   93   92   91   1   2   3   4   5   6   7   8   9   10

DISMANTLING RACISM

"This book is designed successfully for those of us who are white and deeply dismayed by the racism we keep discovering in ourselves and throughout society. It helps us understand how our racism functions in, and is perpetrated in, our homes, schools, churches, and institutions. It is a tough and demanding book that moves us through guilt and blame to effective action. It is particularly helpful for those of us involved in local churches and ecumenical groups who are committed to dismantling racism and are willing to help other white people to change and especially to seek to be changed ourselves."

—JOAN B. CAMPBELL
General Secretary
National Council of the
Churches of Christ in the U.S.A.

"Racism continues to move as a demonic force that threatens the vitality of the church and the promise of a just and free multicultural, multiracial society. Joe Barndt invites readers to participate in a conspiracy led by the Creator along with the poor and oppressed to overcome evil and oppression by tearing down the walls of racism and by building multicultural communities and institutions. *Dismantling Racism* reminds us of the critical role white persons have to play in building a new community."

—CRAIG J. LEWIS
Executive Director
Commission for Multicultural Ministries
Evangelical Lutheran Church in America

"This book needs to be read because it speaks with a clear voice to a major issue of our day, racism. I recommend it to all who are deeply concerned about the evils of racism: to the person who is already sensitive to the issue and is searching for ways to respond; and to the person who needs to become aware of how racism functions and is perpetrated in our homes, schools, churches, and other institutions. This is a book addressed to Christians to help them find ways to change in the struggle against racism and to achieve the goal of freedom for all people."

—CHARLES H. MAAHS
Bishop
Missouri-Kansas Synod
Evangelical Lutheran Church in America

CONTENTS

FOREWORD

As an African American child growing up in Norfolk, Virginia, in the 1940s and 1950s, I was painfully reminded of my place and identity in society by the sign For Whites Only. It was a concrete example of the reality that the land in which I existed was divided into two separate and very unequal societies—one white and one Black—and the boundaries and parameters of these societies were defined by racism. White was affirmed as being genetically superior, the dominant and privileged group with the right to life, liberty, and the pursuit of happiness. Black was described as being genetically inferior, second class citizens, the disenfranchised minority with no rights that whites were bound to respect.

Racism became a life-threatening reality that impacted every facet of my life. It was like an imprisoning cage destroying community, dehumanizing persons, and locking Blacks and whites alike into confrontational roles and identities. It determined what we thought and believed, how we acted and reacted, who we trusted and who we dare not trust.

Racism was not only dehumanizing—it was demonic. When white prejudice was yoked with white power it became a system of exploitation and domination. For Whites Only became the code words for a social, political, and economic system that acted to keep persons in subjugation. Whites controlled the majority of the financial and economic resources, institutions, and levers of power. White power decided who would eat and who would go on city aid when out of work; who went to what schools and who did not go; who had transportation and who didn't; who was arrested and who was not arrested; who was investigated for brutality and murder and who was allowed to go uninvestigated; what neighborhoods were turned down for urban renewal and what neighborhoods were targeted for urban removal and regentrification. The cumulative effect of this form of institutional racism was that it severely limited the opportunity and access of Black people and created a defacto American apartheid system.

As we move toward the twenty-first century, I am clear that racism in the United States is not only an issue between Blacks and whites, it is an issue of power, domination, and control that defines white America's relationship with Native Americans, Hispanics, and Asian Americans. It is further a phenomena that is visible in every part of the world. No nation is totally free of it. Acts of violence, oppression, and subjugation based on color of skin are increasing at an alarming rate producing a litany of shame for all humankind.

Racism is perhaps the major moral issue of the twenty-first century. It weaves a negative web of bigotry, hate, and violence; it makes us all victims in a worldview that is marked by greed, wealth, exploitation, and oppression. It makes us all captives in an imprisoning vision that cannot work and servants to an old world order that must be dismantled. The challenge is to find the way toward an inclusive, pluralistic society that celebrates and affirms the gifts and perspectives of all; to engage in a redistribution of power and resources, and to rebuild a world where racial and economic justice can flow like a mighty stream.

The question is how? This book provides some answers. While the words and visions in these pages have meaning for all of us who are citizens of a global community, it is primarily addressed to whites by one who is himself white. In the introduction to this book the author states clearly:

"This book . . . is written for white people and about white people. . . . It is about our white racial problems. Books about America's racial problems are usually about people of color: African Americans, Native Americans, Asians, and Hispanics. This book is about racial problems, but it is about us, the 'majority people,' and about the problems of our whiteness, especially our problem of white racism."

I applaud one who is willing to stand in his own hometown and announce boldly and confessionally that "the spirit of the Lord is upon him"—freeing him to break rank with an identity and relationships based on privilege and power. Rooted in this confessional, repentance and renewal stance, the author invites whites to examine themselves, their relations, their institutions, and to move from denial to new behavior. This book recognizes the fact that whites have benefited from the structure of racism whether they have ever committed a racist act, uttered a racist word, or uttered a racist thought. Just as surely as African Americans and people of color suffer in a white society because they are African Americans, Native Americans, Hispanics, and Asians, whites benefit because they are white.

If whites have profited from a racist structure they must try to change it—not only for the sake of others—but for the new life and new freedom that can come once one has thrown off the shackles of racism.

While the signs For Whites Only still remain in the cobwebs of my past, my hope for the present and future is centered in the vision I hold for the household of God. This is an inclusive rather than exclusive community. This is a place of nuture and support where individuals are freed to claim new names, new identities, and a renewed sense of purpose in life. In the household of God fear is replaced by love and guilt is transformed into repentance, renewal, reconciliation, and new life.

At the heart of this book is a challenge and a call to Christians in the United States to become the new creation in Christ. The author abandons guilt and blame for a new journey that is empowering and liberating. He insists that the readers become participants rather than spectators by developing their own analysis, their own plan of action, and by creating solutions for an agenda that is still unfinished.

The pages that follow do not present simple definitions or easy answers. The vision and quest, however, is clear: an inclusive pluralistic society. Racism therefore must be faced, denounced, and dismantled. We are still wandering in the wilderness of our past and present. If we can take the first step of the journey, it is possible that we can find our way home.

The Reverend Yvonne V. Delk
Executive Director
Community Renewal Society
Chicago, Illinois

ACKNOWLEDGMENTS

Excerpt from *A Testament of Hope: The Essential Writings of Martin Luther King, Jr.*, edited by James Washington, copyright © 1986 HarperCollins, Publishers, Inc. Reprinted by permission.

Excerpts from *Race, Religion and the Continuing Dilemma* by C. Eric Lincoln. Copyright © 1984 by C. Eric Lincoln. Reprinted by permission of Hill and Wang, a division of Farrar, Straus and Giroux, Inc.

Synopsis of lecture given at Holden Village, August 1989. Reprinted by permission of Dr. Albert Pero.

Excerpts from "Road to Damascus: Kairos and Conversion" in *Kairos: Three Prophetic Challenges to the Church* (Grand Rapids, MI: William B. Eerdmans Publishing Co., 1990). Reprinted by permission of the Center for Concern, Washington, DC.

Excerpts from *Travelling Light* by William McClain, copyright © 1981 Friendship Press, New York. Used by permission.

Excerpts from "Right Wing Religion: Have the Chickens Come Home to Roost?" in *Journal of Theology for Southern Africa*, December 1989, pp. 7-16. Reprinted by permission of the publisher.

Excerpts from speech given by Jim Wallis at convocation on Justice, Peace and Integrity of Creation in Seoul, Korea, March 1990. Reprinted by permission.

Excerpt from *Racial Formation in the United States* by Michael Omi and Howard Winnant, copyright © 1986 Routledge & Kegan Paul. Reprinted by permission of Routledge, Chapman and Hall.

INTRODUCTION

. . . The Right to Life, Liberty, and the
Pursuit of Happiness.
—(U.S. Declaration of Independence)

A Fable

Once upon a time there was a kingdom of people who pursued happiness. Nothing was more important to them than being happy. The happier they became, the happier they wanted to be.

The source of the people's happiness was a magic Happiness Machine. Whenever the people felt unhappy they would pour their troubled feelings into the Happiness Machine. The magic machine would melt their feelings down and purify them. The residue of their troubles became dross, and the dross was drained away and dumped into a distant part of the kingdom. The people would take their purified feelings and go away singing and feeling happy again. The years and centuries went by, and the happy people became happier and happier because of the wonderful effects of the Happiness Machine.

There was only one problem. Another group of people lived in a distant part of the kingdom where all the dross was dumped. The dross made them very unhappy. And the more dross that was dumped, the unhappier they became. Unfortunately, these poor, unhappy people were not permitted to use the

1

Happiness Machine, because the one thing the magic machine could not do was purify its own dross.

The unhappy people complained to the happy people about the problems they had with the dross. But the happy people ignored their complaints. When they were confronted with the terrible results of their happiness, these happy people simply took their troubled feelings to the Happiness Machine and it made them happy again. It was easy to believe that it was not the dross of their own troubles that made other people unhappy. Rather, they convinced themselves that the unhappy people were just incurably unhappy and that they had nobody but themselves to blame for their unhappiness.

It was not long before the unhappy people began to protest more insistently about their situation. They organized marches and demonstrations. They demanded that the dross be removed from their part of the kingdom. And they demanded a fair share of happiness for their people. But the happy people turned a deaf ear to their protests, which only served to make the unhappy people angrier, and they protested all the more.

Finally, the happy people could no longer ignore the protests. They used force to put down the protesters, and arrested and jailed the leaders. They passed laws and organized military force to control the unhappy people. Many of the unhappy people were killed. This only made the others angrier and more unhappy. They began to plot and plan how they could destroy the Happiness Machine.

The conflict and tension caused a severe drain on the happy people's happiness. In addition to everything else, many of them were becoming uneasy about the way the unhappy people were being treated. All these new troubles made the Happiness Machine work even harder, and consequently, even more dross was produced. They had to build an even bigger and better Happiness Machine to take care of the happiness needs of the people; consequently, the dross was piled higher and higher and spread farther and farther into other parts of the kingdom, which made more and more people unhappy and angry. It was not long before the unhappy people were in a constant state of rebellion.

Then a new and even greater danger arose. The Happiness Machine became so large and productive that there was no place on earth left to put the dross. The piles of dross crept closer and closer to the homes of the happy people and to the place where the Happiness Machine was operating. Now the happy people were threatened not only by the rebellion of the unhappy people, but also by their own Happiness Machine.

The new danger caused even greater internal conflict and tension among the happy people. Some wanted to build an even bigger Happiness Machine in order to deal with the crisis they were facing. Others began to see that the Happiness Machine was not the solution to their problems, but the cause. They wanted to reduce the size of the machine, or even dismantle it altogether. Some even began to wish that they could join together with the unhappy people to find solutions to the problem and build a new society together.

———————

The end of this story has not yet been written. This book is an invitation to readers to see themselves as part of the story and to help write its ending.

———————

As the reader has already guessed, this fable is about us and our real-life Happiness Machines. The real Happiness Machines are the structures and institutions of our society. They belong to us, and they work for us. They produce food and clothing, cars and housing, resorts and recreation, law and order. Their purpose is to make us happy.

But our Happiness Machines do not make everyone happy. They produce dross. They produce poverty and segregated ghettos, unemployment and underemployment, and inadequate housing, health, and education. The very same systems that create and sustain our standards of living also create and perpetuate wretched conditions for millions upon millions of people, not only in the United States, but throughout the world as well. This fable is, in fact, no fable at all, but a story about the real world in which you and I live.

The Dross of Racism

The subject of this book is racism. It is among the predominant issues of the 1990s. For more than twenty years, since 1970, this issue seemed to be virtually erased from the consciousness of most people in the United States. But once again it has placed itself dramatically and forcefully on our present-day agendas. Its re-emergence is due partly to the recent increase in racial violence that has been too horrifying to ignore. However, looking beneath the surface, we are confronted with an even uglier reality: that these racial incidents are but the symptoms of a disease in our society that is more serious than ever—the disease of racism.

Many, perhaps most of us, were hoping that problems of racial injustice in the United States had been sufficiently dealt with in the 1960s, when the civil rights movement drew to a close. We believed—or wanted to believe—that the social conditions of people of color,[1] such as housing, education, employment, and health, would now be improving. We believed—or wanted to believe—that the increasing numbers of people of color in elected offices, media programming, and other public positions were a sign that things were truly changing. But now it is becoming clear that these changes were more illusory than real. Moreover, as is indicated by the growing number of racial incidents, white society hasn't changed much either. Racism still plagues not only the individual attitudes and behavior of white people, but, even more seriously, the public systems and institutions of white society.

The purpose of this book is to examine racism as it exists in the United States in the 1990s. We will explore the ways in which it has changed over the past few decades as well as the ways in which it has remained the same. Most important, we will focus on the task of dismantling racism, how we can work to bring it to an end and replace it with a racially just, multiracial, multicultural society.

Not the Only Form of Dross

Although the particular focus of this book is racism, we need to recognize from the outset that racism is not the only social evil in our society. The dross of our Happiness Machines produces other problems, such as sexism, classism, nationalism, militarism, and environmental pollution, all of which cause tremendous suffering and endanger humanity's existence. For the purpose of this book, the happy people in our fable represent U.S. white society, and the unhappy people represent people of color who suffer from white racism. Even as we focus on the single issue of racism, however, we must be aware that all these issues are interwoven and that their solutions are interdependent.

As this book progresses it should become clear that racism affects nearly every aspect of our lives. Wherever one goes, whatever stone is overturned in the field of social turmoil, whatever the issue, one encounters the persistent, ever-present problem of racism. An understanding of racism is needed, therefore, not only by those who are directly involved in issues of racial justice, but also by those who work with all the other issues of justice and social change.

A Book for White People

This book on racism is addressed primarily to a white audience. It is written for white people and about white people, and it is written by a white person. It is about our white racial problems. Books about America's racial problems are usually about people of color: African Americans, Native Americans, Asians, and Hispanics. This book is about racial problems, but it is about us, the "majority people," and about the problems of our whiteness, especially our problem of white racism.

With the exception of the first chapter, there is very little in this book about the results of racism—that is, about the effects of racism as they are experienced by people of color. The central focus is, rather, on the reality of racism itself as it exists in white people and in the institutions, communities, and culture of white society. The goal of the book is, above all, to help white people understand how racism functions and is perpetuated in our homes, schools, churches, and other institutions. An equally important goal is to help equip white people to combat and dismantle racism effectively and to help build a multiracial, multicultural society.

In South Africa, the churches use the phrase, "mission to white people," to describe the responsibility of helping prepare white people for inevitable change in that country.[2] We can apply the same phrase to our situation here. As the phrase implies, we need to begin working for change in our situation. When Jesus sent his disciples "into all the world," he was not just sending them on a mission to a distant community or to foreign lands. The world begins where we are. We have a mission to our own people. If we see ourselves already in the process of change, we have the responsibility to help others onto the same path.

In order to carry out this mission to our own people, we have a lot to learn about racism and how it works. This entails unlearning false understandings, relearning and correcting our history, and developing new perspectives with which to address the world in which we live. Even more important, in the simplest of terms, we need to learn to love our own people in a new way. If we are to be prepared for mission to white people, we must discover in ourselves a desire to be in new community with our own people as well as with all people in a multiracial, multicultural world.

In addition to being addressed to a white audience, this book is addressed even more particularly to Christians in the United States. While our aim is to help Christians and non-Christians alike to understand racism, our particular emphasis is on equipping Christians to dismantle racism in church and society. Our churches are not strangers to the task of combating racism. So much of what we have done, however, has been too little too late. We have not yet made a serious impact on the racism that surrounds us or is within us. It is hoped that this book will make some small contribution to our next assault on the demonic evil of racism.

One other word of introduction: the approach of this book is not based on accusations or blame, nor does it seek to produce guilt. The primary thesis about racism is that we are all—people of color and white people alike—indoctrinated and socialized in such a way as to be made into "prisoners of racism." Every leader in the struggle against racism, from Frederick Douglass to Dr. Martin Luther King Jr. has emphasized that racism is as debilitating to white people as it is to people of color, and that the goal of freedom is for all people.

On the other hand, although it is hoped that the reader will not feel attacked and overburdened with guilt and blame, the goal of this book is to be tough and demanding. No simple definitions or easy answers will be found here. Moreover, there is an insistence that readers participate by developing their own analysis and plans for action. It is assumed that readers not only seek to be equipped to carry out a mission that will help other white people to change but also seek to be changed themselves.

Writing an Ending to the Story

What kind of conclusion would we write for our fable? A number of different endings are possible. In traditional fairy tales, the perpetuators of evil are destroyed and the heroes and heroines live happily ever after. We are not dealing here with a fairy tale, however, but with a story reflecting real life. The destruction of the perpetuators of evil is not the goal of those who are victims of its racial oppression. The goal is freedom for all people—people of color and white people alike.

In considering an ending to this story, the triumphal victory of one side over the other is not the most frightening or dangerous scenario. The greatest danger is self-destruction brought about by the greed of the happy people and their control of the Happiness Machine. The most frightening ending of all is one in which those who possess power over the magic machines and who derive exclusive benefit from them go to their deaths clinging uselessly to their machines, their world views, and their pretense about reality. Such a terrifying conclusion to the story precludes any hope of transformation and change.

Of course, many people are quite convinced that such an unhappy ending would be both realistic and inevitable. This is the belief of many of the world's poor, unhappy people. They experience the predominantly white majority in the United States as people who refuse to change, as people who refuse to relinquish or even share the reins of power and the goods of the earth. Furthermore, they see us as totally unwilling to acknowledge that we benefit from and even depend upon the sufferings of others for our happiness.

Even a person as committed to change as Dr. Martin Luther King Jr. often worried whether the white society was capable of making the necessary changes to avoid destruction of our civilization:

> Racism can well be that corrosive evil that will bring down the curtain on Western Civilization. Arnold Toynbee has said that some twenty-six civilizations have risen from the face of the earth. Almost all of them have descended into the junk heaps of destruction. The decline and fall of these civilizations, according to Toynbee, was not caused by external invasions but by internal decay. They failed to respond creatively to the challenges impinging upon them. If Western civilization does not respond constructively to the challenge to banish racism, some future historian will have to say that a great civilization died because it lacked the soul and commitment to make justice a reality for all. . . .[3]

The Struggle for a Just Ending

On the other hand, Dr. King was not usually pessimistic. He held onto an undying faith in God and a belief in the power of good to triumph over evil. It is this same belief that informs the fundamental assumptions of this book. Millions of people in the United States are involved in efforts to write an ending to our story. Through their teaching, protesting, advocating, mobilizing, and organizing for political and social change, they express their conviction that the Happiness Machine can be dismantled, or that the system that controls the machine can be transformed and that the machine can be redirected to serve everyone on an equal and just basis. They believe that those who are now in power will yet be able to read the signs of the times, and yield their power rather than bring about their own destruction.

Not just in the United States but all around the world similar efforts are being made to do this very same thing, to write a just ending to this story. Perhaps the most dramatic of all these efforts is in South Africa, where as these lines are being written, a great risk is being taken by the Black majority of that country. Black South Africans are risking that the powerful and oppressively racist white minority that controls the government can be made to change direction before it is too late, that it will give up control of the country rather than face total civil war. The same drama is taking place on every continent in the world. Almost everywhere, people are trying to write the conclusion to the story of the Happiness Machine.

This book is written especially for such people as these. Its primary task is not to convert those who still believe in Happiness Machines. Rather, it is aimed toward those who already believe that a just ending to the story is possible and who need to be better equipped to carry out this task of conversion and change. There is, of course, a great need to convince and convert those who still believe in the lies and fantasies of racism and racial privilege. We who have ourselves been led by others to new understandings must realize how important it is that others receive similar help from us. This book has been written to equip us for this and other tasks related to the writing of a just ending to the story.

1

THE CONTINUING EVIL
OF RACISM

---

*But while everybody was asleep, an enemy
came and sowed weeds among the wheat, and
then went away.*
—Matthew 13:25

Racism is an evil weed sown in the garden of humanity. It has
grown wildly, entangling the healthy plants and covering the
pathways, creating a great maze, a labyrinth with twists and turns
that have led humanity astray. Racism has entwined and en-
trapped us all.

Before we begin to define and dissect racism in our
present day, it is essential to realize how deeply the roots of racism are embedded and intertwined in the life and history of the
United States. From its earliest days, the seeds were sown and
this evil plant has grown and flourished. It is clearly evident in
the genocide of Native Americans, in the enslavement of Africans, and in the drafting of a constitution that reserved and guar-
anteed the precious fruits of freedom almost exclusively for European immigrants.

As the decades and centuries passed, the roots of racism
remained strong, sending up fresh shoots each season. With chill-
ing regularity, to this very day, new crops of racial violence and
death are harvested in the streets and alleys of U.S. cities and in
the dusty lanes of our rural countryside. Each time this undesir-

able harvest manifests itself, our nation's leaders express their moral outrage and indignation. Then, nodding in agreement and pledging to prevent its recurrence, we forget that it ever happened, guaranteeing thereby that it will happen again and again, just as surely as seedtime turns to harvest.

With this pattern we passed through the eighteenth and nineteenth centuries and are now nearly through the twentieth century as well. Each time a particularly horrible phase of racial turmoil breaks out, we pretend at its passing that we have finally achieved racism's defeat and death. And we pretend to be newly surprised when, months or years later, another and another and still another shoot of the evil plant emerges, promising a greater harvest than ever.

And so today, in the final decade of the twentieth century, we have become alarmed once again at the persistent evil of racism. The daily headlines assert its reality. The evening news assaults our consciences. New names and places become household words, and a new geography lesson is taught, from the wanton killings of African Americans in New York City's Howard Beach and Bensonhurst, to the slaughter of Asians in Stockton, California; from senseless police brutality videotaped in Los Angeles, to violent campaigns against Native Americans in Wisconsin. A collage of names, places, facts, and figures reshapes our consciousness. Words and phrases like "regentrification" and "permanent underclass" become part of a new vocabulary, created to explain the current racial situation. The latest graphs, charts, and surveys demonstrate once again that little has changed for the better and much has taken a turn for the worse.

A Path Cut Through the Weeds

For every action there is a reaction. Racism's persistence is only half the story. The other half is tireless and heroic resistance by the victims. A tenacious struggle for racial justice in this country has been a part of our history almost from the start. Through the courageous efforts of millions of sisters and brothers who lived before our time, a path was cut through the maze of racism. This is the very same path that we are now struggling to maintain and widen. To understand more fully our place in history as we gather at the end of the twentieth century, joining our efforts to combat racism and build a multicultural church and society, we need to acknowledge and celebrate those who have been on this path before us.

In doing so, we affirm that we are not the first, nor are we alone. Many have been here before us. Those of us now gathered to help write an ending to the story of the Happiness Machines should be aware of those before us as well as those gathering with us today in various parts of the world. God created all people to be free. Again and again it has been demonstrated that, at the very moment of their subjugation and oppression, God inspires people to survive, to resist, and to work for liberation.

There are, of course, long periods when it seems that evil has triumphed; that those who control the chains and shackles will never yield. This was the experience of the Hebrew people who endured and survived enslavement in Egypt for more than 300 years. And then, at last, they heard the words of liberation that God spoke to Moses:

> I have also heard the groaning of the Israelites whom the Egyptians are holding as slaves, and I have remembered my covenant. Say therefore to the Israelites, 'I am the Lord, and I will free you from the burdens of the Egyptians and deliver you from slavery to them. I will redeem you with an outstretched arm and with mighty acts of judgment. I will take you as my people, and I will be your God. You shall know that I am the Lord your God, who has freed you from the burden of the Egyptians. (Exodus 6:5-7)

Throughout history this same confession of faithfulness and deep belief in the final outcome of liberation has been the rallying cry, the quiet encouraging voice, and the preacher's theme for virtually every people under oppression and in enslavement. The following excerpt from a sermon by Dr. Martin Luther King Jr. during the Montgomery bus boycott is an example. Though uniquely beautiful in its formulation and classic in its style, it is not intended to be original in its content. Rather, it illustrates this oft-repeated confession of faith:

The universe is on the side of justice. It says to those who struggle for justice, "You do not struggle alone, but God struggles with you." This belief that God is on the side of truth and justice comes down to us from the long tradition of our Christian faith. There is something at the very center of our faith which reminds us that Good Friday may occupy the throne for the day, but ultimately it must give way to the triumphant beat of the drums of Easter. Evil may so shape events that Caesar will occupy a palace and Christ a cross, but one day that same Christ will rise up and split history into A.D. and B.C., so that even the life of Caesar must be dated by his name. There is something in the universe which justifies Carlyle in saying, "No lie can live forever." There is something in this universe which justifies William Cullen Bryant in saying, "Truth, crushed to earth, will rise again." There is something in this universe that justifies James Russell Lowell in saying: Truth forever on the scaffold / Wrong forever on the throne / Yet that scaffold sways the future / And behind the dim unknown / stands God within the shadows / keeping watch above his own.

And so here in Montgomery, even after more than eleven months, we can walk and never get weary, because we know there is a great camp meeting in the promised land of freedom and justice.[1]

Our history books rarely inform us that when genocidal acts against Native Americans and the importation of African slaves began, there also began a powerful resistance against these evils. Courageous and determined women and men confronted "danger, toils, and snares" to demand the end of racial oppression. When history's pages are accurately written, they will be filled with the names and deeds of these women and men who rebelled against slavery, who resisted Native American exploitation and the theft of native lands, and who rose up again and again to protest the desolation and death caused by white America.

Likewise, it is important to remember and celebrate that such acts of resistance were carried out not only by red, yellow, brown, and black people. A role was also played by a significant number of white people who were convicted by conscience and could not tolerate the racist acts of their fellow whites. In the underground railroad, for example, white station operators worked closely with Black conductors in guiding runaway slaves to freedom. Likewise, white abolitionists and Black leaders of slave rebellions inspired each other to greater acts of courage. The number of white people involved in these activities was not large, and their participation in the resistance cannot erase the reality of direct oppression nor the acquiescence to racism by the majority of whites. However, those who did join the resistance are a crucially important symbol and model for those who would follow their example today.

The Civil Rights Movement: The Path Widens

The greatest effort in cutting a path through the labyrinth of racism in the United States occurred in the lifetime of many readers of this book. This was the civil rights movement. It is amazing to realize that little more than thirty years ago, a legal apartheid system—U.S. style—was still intact and controlled the lives of all people of color in the United States. Separate and unequal education was still the law of the land. Voting was blocked by an array of legal barriers. Housing and the use of all public accommodations was strictly segregated. Even though slavery had been abolished a full century before the civil rights movement, every African American was, for all practical purposes, still in chains. And most Native Americans, Hispanics, and Asians were subjected to similar laws.

Future generations must not be allowed to forget the scenes of hundreds of thousands of people rising up to protest, march, and demonstrate, to face police, dogs, firehoses, and gunfire, to accept the punishment of prison, torture, and death. In what now seems a series of sudden and miraculous events culminating in a few strokes of the pen, the oppressive legal system of segregation that had been carefully constructed during the course of a century was eradicated.[2]

Today there is a great debate about the accomplishments of the civil rights movement and about the progress or lack thereof in the years that followed. We dare not be naive about the movement's failures or about the new forms of racism that have emerged. However, we cannot ignore the movement's victories or fail to learn from this remarkable resistance so recent in our history. During the years of the civil rights movement, followed by a few additional years when civil rights legislation and the War on Poverty began to be implemented, millions of people in and outside of government affirmed that they wanted the future to look different from the past. During a brief, almost Camelot-like moment, all the branches of government—executive, legislative, and judicial—demonstrated what could be accomplished if the will was there.

It didn't last long. The sense of progress was short-lived. However, a number of doors were opened during that one brief moment, creating new opportunities for people of color—opportunities in education, jobs, housing, and politics. Thousands walked through these doors, many of which were all too soon slammed shut again. And many people are still pushing through the doors that remain open. Their efforts have significantly increased the size of the minority middle class, and these people represent a new and potentially powerful leadership for the future. Educators, communicators, business people, social scientists, political leaders—the importance of this new generation of highly skilled people is just beginning to be felt.

One clear example of their presence is in the increased numbers of elected and appointed political leaders, especially in our larger cities. The effect of high concentrations of people of color in these often ghettoized cities has been to create an electorate in which the "racial minority" has become a strong political majority. As a result, to an increasing extent, political leaders, particularly from the African American and Hispanic communities, are taking charge of our city halls.

While celebrating these gains, some important qualifications must be noted. In his book *Race, Religion and the Continuing American Dilemma*, C. Eric Lincoln comments on the dubious power of Blacks in city hall:

> The black mayor is a symbol, a hopeful sign of the potential power of the black electorate. But if that power were miraculously doubled or even tripled it would still be potential and there would be no dramatic improvement in the life of

the masses who inhabit the ghetto. When the available patronage has been divided and dispensed, the Blacks who benefit substantially will be few in number, and the black masses, whose circumstance are the most desolate and the most desperate, will generally remain beyond the effective reach of the most conscientious black mayor. . . . Who then runs the runners while the runners are running the city? Or, to put it another way, what is the power behind the political power that keeps things the way they were? The Blacks in city hall are an important development toward America's political maturation. Their presence is the best evidence of the political direction the struggle for full freedom must take. But that struggle must ultimately receive ratification from those sources which operate above and beyond the sound and the fury of politics and from which most politicians are required to take their cues.[3]

Whether in city hall, university, church, or business, the crucial issue is whether this new leadership will be in a position to help carry forward the struggle for racial justice, or whether it will be co-opted and assimilated into the mainstream of United States politics, rendering it unable to affect the destiny of the many who are still trapped by poverty and powerlessness. For, as we shall see, the civil rights movement and the years that followed are not measured primarily by stories of success but by setbacks and failures.

Once More the Path Is Hidden

For a while, it did seem as if things were moving forward. Despite resistance, despite violence and death, by 1970 a fairly wide swath had been carved through the poisonous weeds of racism. Then, as the protest marches receded into the background, many people assumed that the legislative and judicial apparatus that had created important new legislation in response to insistent demands of the demonstrators would pick up the pace and carry their efforts to completion.

It didn't happen. The nation began to balk. We grew tired of civil rights, tired of the Vietnam war, tired of the anti-war protesters, tired of being challenged and confronted. The elected leaders of the United States said, in effect, "We've had enough." Tragically, they didn't know they had barely begun.

Imperceptibly at first, and then with alarming speed, the path was once again choked with the weeds of racism. The voters elected leaders who would, through active decisions and passive neglect, reverse the forward motion. All the branches of government that, just a few years earlier, had appeared ready to do the right thing, now seemed to coalesce and conspire on how they might do the wrong thing. The Supreme Court, well on its way to becoming the "Reagan Court," announced a series of decisions that undermined the effects of earlier hard-won victories. Bit by bit, decision by decision, they stripped away the power behind legislation affecting school integration, affirmative action, and other steps taken to eliminate discrimination. In 1989, looking back upon the wreckage of more than a decade of judicial deconstruction, Dr. Benjamin Hooks, Executive Director of the National Association for the Advancement of Colored People, described the Supreme Court as "hell-bent on destroying the few gains that women and minorities have made."[4]

More than adequate documentation tracing the deterioration of race relations and racial justice since the civil rights movement is provided by a series of studies and surveys conducted at the end of the 1980s and the beginning of the current decade.[5] These studies reveal that the basic living and working conditions for people of color as compared to whites have, on average, stagnated or deteriorated. The studies also document a dramatic rise in racial prejudice and bigotry. The government's neglect and retreat throughout the 1970s and 1980s seems to have made acceptable the public expression of white resentment and hostility directed against people of color. From working-class communities to university settings, racial incidents have continued to escalate.

The effect of the nation's betrayal has been most devastating for those who are condemned to live below the poverty level. In the late 1970s, the United States was confronted with a serious recession. And, although the poor were required to do most of the belt-tightening, they were less affected than any other group by the recovery in the early 1980s. Ten years later, in the early 1990s, the poorest 25 percent of the nation, particularly people of color in the inner cities and rural areas, still remained in deep recession and depression.

Government programs of social service and development for the poor also seemed to come to a halt during the 1980s. During the fiscal years 1980-1990, while government funding for the military increased by 37 percent, it decreased by an average of 40 percent for low income housing, low income employment services, child care, health care for migrants, and maternal and child health.[6] The result: conditions are no better and are in many ways worse than before the civil rights movement and the War on Poverty. Although unemployment rates have dropped dramatically in the main part of the population, unemployment and underemployment rates in inner-city communities of color have skyrocketed, reaching 50 percent to 70 percent for those most affected: young men from 18 to 30 years of age. In 1989, surveys of the chronically poor in eight major cities found that 61 percent had not held a job in the preceding two years, and that 44 percent had never held a job or had any job training.[7] Other statistics released in 1990 reveal that nearly 25 percent of Black young men were either in jail, on probation, or on parole.[8]

The increasing depression of inner-city ghetto populations is characterized by escalating alcohol and drug addiction, the AIDS epidemic, school dropouts, unemployment, internalized violence, poor health, and early death. Drugs are no longer simply a crime problem but in many areas define a community's culture and economy totally beyond the control of authorities. The glazed look in many people's eyes, however, is less drug-induced than a mark of utter hopelessness.

In a public hearing on the drug epidemic in the African American community, one woman cried for help to save the next generation. But the next spokesperson, in even greater despair, gave the following testimony: "The next generation is already lost," she said. "It is their children, my grandchildren, that we may have some opportunity still left to do something about."

The "Permanent" Underclass

The newest and perhaps most ominous sign is the apparent readiness of our nation's leaders to write off a significant portion of our citizens without even the pretense of trying to effect change. In the mid-1980s, a new phrase, "the permanent underclass," was created to describe those people at the bottom of the economic ladder for whom any hope of recovery had been abandoned.[9] Already by the end of the decade, it was common for government officials to refer to the "reality of a permanent underclass living amidst general prosperity."[10]

Accepting the permanence of economic deprivation in the United States is an entirely new and enormously dangerous step. Though previous social and economic programs have made little or no progress toward eliminating the poverty that has plagued more than 25 percent of our population, there has always been at least the assumption that recovery and change are possible. The acceptance of "permanent underclass" status for a significant portion of the population living at bare survival levels, and the concession that economic recovery is for them no longer even a goal, are the kinds of situations heretofore recognized as existing only in third world countries. The recognition that such "third world"[11] conditions exist in the United States is another tragic indicator of our current situation.

And so we are faced with the reality that the path has grown over, and has once again become almost impenetrable. Once again the escalation of racism in America has reached a point of crisis. The analysts and prophets are repeating their forecasts of earlier years, of increasing spirals of racial violence, unabating tension, and long hot summers. As we set out in this book to find a new sense of direction, we are forced to draw three unavoidable conclusions about our current situation:

1. Racism continues to infect and affect nearly every area of our national life. Past efforts to change and improve this situation have been inadequate and incomplete. For the most part, racism has become more deeply im-

bedded, more carefully disguised, and more difficult to eradicate.

2. The separation between white America and America's people of color has widened, and the tension has deepened, producing in communities of color a greater sense of despair and abandonment than ever and a growing identification with nations of the third world.

3. We are being inexorably drawn toward a new period of confrontation and conflict, as the historical cycle once again follows its pattern of hope and anticipation, succeeded by disappointment and despair, followed by anger and protest. This pattern has not changed in centuries.

What does it mean for the United States to be faced with a new cycle of conflict and confrontation? On the one hand, it may be seen as a depressing repetition of history, holding little promise or possibility. On the other hand, it may be perceived as the sign of an awakening to new opportunities for struggle and change. It depends on where we stand. For those who have hoped and prayed for an end to complacency and longed for a new commitment to racial justice in America, these are not so much indications of defeat as they are opportunities for a new beginning.

A new beginning for America starts with racial justice. Looking back at the last twenty years of reversals and regression, looking at the present moment of terrifying increase in racial bigotry and violence, and looking ahead to God's call for a new moment in history, it is time for us to turn once again to the reopening and creating of a yet wider path, a broad highway of justice through the maze of racism in America.

Contexts for a New Beginning

As we start down this path once again, we can recognize that things have changed since the last time. The 1990s are very different from the 1960s. The circles of history do not have to be vicious cycles in which we are condemned to face the same problems and make the same mistakes over and over again. We are building on the accomplishments of past struggles. There are at least five ways in which the situation has changed, providing new contexts and new definitions for our struggle.

1. *Racism is against the law.* Until very recently, there were very few laws in the United States against racism. To the contrary, before the 1960s, the law required that people behave in racist ways. During the civil rights movement, the only weapon against racism was moral pressure. Now, the laws that protected racism have for the most part been removed, and an entirely new set of laws against racism has been created. Even though these laws are still being tested, and are not being effectively implemented, racism is, nevertheless, illegal. Laws and policies against racism exist not only in our federal, state, and city governments, but also in most corporations, business and industry, and in unions, universities, and churches.

   Clearly, however, the law is not yet being obeyed. Racism still thrives and prospers. Yet several things have been gained. In the first place, a legal standard against which the existence of racism can be measured is beginning to emerge. Second, continuing racism exposes an internal contradiction in our legal structure. Society's own laws are being disobeyed, not just the laws of religion or the dismissible moral imperative of a liberal fringe. Ultimately, if a society based on law is to survive, it will enforce its laws and protect those victimized by the violation of those laws. Therefore, we who work to eliminate racism in the United States have a new and powerful weapon with which to accomplish our goals: racism is against the law.

2. *The central focus is on economics.* Once the battle against segregation and discrimination in public accommodations was won, a far more serious problem needed to be

addressed: racism in economics. A popular expression says it all: "It doesn't help to have the right to eat in a restaurant if you can't afford the prices on the menu." Economics has always been at the core of racism. The elimination of segregation and discrimination in public accommodations and at the voting booth were necessary first steps. But they were merely preludes to the more central struggle against segregation and discrimination in the marketplace. In the following chapters the reader will discover that this issue, above all others, defines the direction of efforts to confront and eliminate racism. Tyrone Pitts of the National Council of Churches writes:

> Although the historical development of racism in America is well documented, most historians do not connect the dynamics of racism with the dynamics of the U.S. economic system. . . . Today, racism and economics are more tightly interwoven than ever. For non-European Americans, the economic forecast is grim.[12]

3. *Culture is important,* both in combating racism and in building a multiracial, multicultural society. This is, in a sense, the new frontier in the struggle for racial justice. Until now, the issue of culture has been superseded by the more immediate priorities of political and economic justice. Furthermore, the overwhelming dominance of the European cultural heritage in the United States has prevented by sheer force the evolution of an alternate vision for a multicultural society.

Now, however, dramatic new possibilities are inherent in the recognition that, as the United States enters a new century, the white population will soon no longer be the majority. The old myth of the melting pot, long outmoded, can now also be outvoted. As we shall explore in greater detail, our efforts to combat racism in America will lead us to an exciting new frontier: the building of a truly multiracial and multicultural society.

4. *Racism is a global issue.* It is increasingly obvious that all nations of the world are politically and economically interconnected. No nation is an island. Each country takes its place in the community of nations, either by contributing to or by acting to prevent the solutions to one another's problems.

In this context, racism in the United States is linked to and inseparable from racism and other forms of oppression and suffering throughout the world. It is particularly linked to the struggle against apartheid in South Africa. Most nations of the third world still suffer from the long-term effects of Euroamerican colonialism. Economically, a "global apartheid" can no longer be ignored or excused. No longer can a small white minority be permitted to maintain itself with incredible privilege at the expense of the nonwhite majority. The resolution of racial issues within individual countries, including our own, can no longer be dealt with in isolation from global issues of racial injustice.

5. *The leadership role of people of color.* Unfortunately, we who are white often find this easier to comprehend intellectually than to follow in practice. Yet it is the crucial area in this listing of contexts for a new beginning. The priorities of white people in achieving racial justice are often quite different from those that are defined by people of color. Throughout this book, the reader should assign the greatest possible weight to those points that have as their aim a stronger commitment by whites to follow the strength and leadership of people of color.

It should be reemphasized now that the perspective of this book is not despair, but hope. The basis for this hope is not so much a belief in the potential of white people to change themselves, but, rather, in the strength and leadership of people of color. Even though our society has given up on the poor, and especially poor people of color, we can be sure of two things: first, that God has not given up on the poor, and second, that the poor have not given up on themselves. Someone may have called them the "permanent underclass," but that is a name chosen neither by God nor the poor themselves.

History shows that when people are pushed to the bottom, they refuse to stay there. From the time when Moses led the uprising of the Hebrews, through the rebellion of oppressed people all over the world in our own day, those who are stripped of dignity and their basic human rights will rise in strength, demanding that which God has promised to all people. In the short term, systems of political and economic oppression often succeed in their objectives by turning the anger and frustration of a people inward upon themselves. The greatest violence usually does not come directly from the oppressor but from internalized anger and self-hatred of the oppressed. Eventually this anger turns outward once again—as indeed it should—and focuses on the real cause of suffering, either through organized disobedience and rebellion, or through a rage born of desperation.

The ultimate hope for the United States and the rest of the world is that the poor and oppressed will develop the degree of strength and leadership that will lead to a better world. More specifically, the hope for white America, as well as the entire white western world, is that we will be able to relinquish our power and control, and write a positive ending for our fable before it is too late. Not only because we're running out of time, not only because we're afraid of what will happen if we don't change, but also because it is right, because it is just, and because it is the will of God.

As Christians we know that a new ending for the story is already being written. In the birth, death, and resurrection of Jesus we see that the promise is being fulfilled—the reconciliation of all creation with God, and of all people with each other. How long it will be before this is fully accomplished is known only to the mind of God. However, each of us has a part to play in bringing it to completion. All people of every nation, of every racial and ethnic background, are called to participate in bringing this story to a just and peaceful conclusion.

2

WHAT IS WHITE RACISM?

The same fetters that bind the captive
bind the captor.
—*C. Eric Lincoln*

"I'm not a racist, but . . . ," claims a person talking about his racial beliefs.

"The police have determined that the crime was not an incident of racism," reads a quote from a newspaper article.

"But it isn't a problem of racism; it's an economic problem," argues a person in a debate about racial issues.

"Blacks can be just as racist as whites," claims a university student who has experienced Black/white conflict on campus.

"Reverse racism" is charged in a lawsuit by a white person as the reason she did not get a job.

To begin with, we need a common understanding of what we mean by racism. As the above examples demonstrate, the word is used in many confusing and contradictory ways. To develop an analysis of racism, we must create a clear definition that will be used consistently throughout this book. The goal of this chapter is to explore several components of such a definition. Together they comprise the understanding of racism that will be further developed in later chapters.

A definition must correspond to that which is being defined. It can be very tempting to oversimplify or to avoid some of the more painful and difficult aspects of racism. Our definition must reflect adequately and accurately the historical and present-day realities described in the previous chapter. We need a definition that encompasses the terrible destructiveness of racism as a national and global evil, yet includes the single racist act of one individual or the suffering of a single victim. Our definition must take into account racism's resistance to change as well as those situations in which it is being overcome. Our definition must clearly describe racism's causes and unflinchingly name those responsible for it, while being inviting to those who wish to work for its elimination. Finally, our definition must leave room for debate and disagreement on the part of the reader; at the same time, the reader should expect, indeed insist, that it be consistently applied. It is a tall order. Let us see how close we come to fulfilling it.

Racism Is Prejudice Plus Power

Let us begin with a working definition of racism, and then explore the definition's implications. Racism is clearly more than simple prejudice or bigotry. Everyone is prejudiced, but not everyone is racist. To be prejudiced means to have opinions without knowing the facts and to hold onto those opinions, even after contrary facts are known. To be racially prejudiced means to have distorted opinions about people of other races. Racism goes beyond prejudice. It is backed up by power. Racism is the power to enforce one's prejudices. More simply stated, racism is prejudice plus power.

All of us, white people and people of color, are racially prejudiced. We have been taught, or have developed by ourselves, distorted and unsubstantiated opinions about people from other racial and ethnic backgrounds. And we don't give up these prejudices easily. Often, we vigorously resist alternate points of view that conflict with our distorted racial biases. However, serious and damaging as it surely is, prejudice or bigotry is still not the same as racism. Racial bigotry is terribly painful, to say the least. I do not like to be prejudged because I am European

American, any more than others like to be prejudged because they are African American, Native American, Hispanic, or Asian. At the same time, a prejudiced person's distortions have only limited negative effect. It is something like the well-known child's rebuke of nasty name-calling: "Sticks and stones will break my bones, but names will never hurt me." Even though the name-calling of racial prejudice is profoundly destructive and hurtful, it is far worse when backed up by force, violent or otherwise. Racial prejudice is transformed into racism when one racial group becomes so powerful and dominant that it is able to control another group and to enforce the controlling group's biases.

A Question of Power

The issue here is power and its misuse. Power is, of course, in itself neither good nor evil. Whether power becomes good or evil depends on who has it and how it is used. Power is especially dangerous when used to control the lives of others. This is racism's power. It is not only the control of one individual over another, but also a collective power expressed through political and economic systems, through educational, cultural, religious, and other societal institutions. It victimizes entire racial or ethnic groups for the purpose of maintaining the benefits and privileges of another group.

Racism (prejudice plus power) develops when personal opinion and individual bigotry are codified and enforced as societal behavior. Racism structures a society so that the prejudices of one racial group are taught, perpetuated, and enforced to the benefit of the dominant group. Racism harnesses the energies and loyalties of the dominant group for that group's purposes. Racism provides better service and facilities for the dominant group through that group's institutions. Racism decrees more severe restrictions and control over its victims than it does over the dominant group.

A helpful method of analyzing the power of racism has been developed by an anti-racism training organization in New Orleans, the People's Institute for Survival and Beyond. The method, called the "Big Foot Analysis" is described here as used by the People's Institute in a workshop setting. First of all, a typical ghetto community of African Americans or other people of color is portrayed, with all its problems, troubles, conditions of suffering, and struggles for survival. Then, the participants in the discussion are asked to name the feet that are "kicking this community in the behind," that is, what structures and powers determine the life of the community? And how much control and participation does the community have in these powers and structures?

Participants are amazed by the list of "feet"—the institutions, organizations, bureaucracies, and structures, as well as the way their power is exercised almost exclusively from outside the community. It turns out that nearly every aspect of life in poor racial ghettos is orchestrated by outside institutions that kick the community in the behind. All of them combined are the "big feet" of power.[1]

C. Eric Lincoln describes vividly the powerlessness of those who experience the "big foot" in their daily lives in the African American ghetto:

> Each morning all over America the great American tragedy was reenacted each time a black man looked at himself in a mirror as he shaved, and each time a black woman put on the face she would wear in her efforts to find bread for her family in the kitchens of the elegant houses far from the decaying flats and tenements of the racial compound to which she was assigned. What each saw in the looking glass was a cipher citizen—an American who would have no serious input in any of the decisions which would determine the quality of his or her significant experiences for that day, or any day; whose life chances had already been programmed with sinister predictability by persons unknown, or, even if known, unavailable and unconcerned. . . .
>
> Freedom implies power—*the power to be responsible.* Such power was unthinkable because black responsibility lay well beyond what liberal white America envisioned when it endorsed the black mission to overcome. The power that shaped life in the black ghetto was not, and is not, of course, black power. It does not originate in the ghetto. It is power from the outside. It is alien power, with many faces. It is the nonresident merchants who come into the ghetto with

the sun in the morning and who leave with the sun in the evening, taking with them the day's toll for their visitation. It is also the vexatious blue presence—that alien anonymous, contemptuous phalanx known as "the law" but more often than not considered an army of occupation pursuing its own private system of spoils. It is the ubiquitous presence of alien school teachers, case workers, process servers, rent collectors, repossessors, bailiffs, political hustlers, and assorted functionaries and racketeers whose economic stakes in the black ghetto require their temporary and grudging presence imposed upon a community they detest and which detests them in return.[2]

Racism's New Power to Delude

Racism can be expressed with an iron fist or with a velvet glove. At its coarsest and most unsophisticated, racism uses violence to enforce explicit laws to subjugate and control. Examples of such racism are the practice of slavery in the United States, the genocide of Jews in Nazi Germany, and the system of apartheid in South Africa. The evil of such blatant racism is obvious.

Racism also assumes sophisticated forms that depend less on brute force than on psychological methods that dissipate resistance. In such forms, racism may in fact create the illusion that it does not exist and therefore be far more difficult to detect and eliminate. Yet its power to oppress is no less than that of open and blatant racism. Iron fist or velvet glove, the results are the same.

For example, under a blatant form of racism, laws explicitly dictate where members of the subjugated race can live, the limits of their education, and the kind of work they must do. As a result, they are undereducated, underemployed, and ghettoized. However, under a more sophisticated system of racism, members of the same race have no explicit restrictions on where they live, no legal limitations on their education, nor on the kind of jobs they can have. Yet, they are still undereducated, underemployed, and ghettoized. It is, of course, emphatically denied that racism exists, but it obviously does exist because of the observable results. It is this sophisticated form that racism has taken in the United States, particularly during the past thirty years, and that we are seeking to describe and define in this book.

If racism is prejudice plus power, then contemporary racism's greatest power is this ability to create illusions and delude victims and perpetrators alike. It deludes the victims into believing that their rulers have only their best interests at heart. It deludes the dominant group into believing that it is not racist, that it is treating its victims well, and that there is no need to change. This power to create illusions is devastating, for it provides justification to the dominant group for its actions. A few more examples may be helpful here.

We have already seen the illusion that is created when racism is described simply in terms of personal prejudice and individual bigotry. As we discussed a few pages earlier, such an understanding of racism does not begin to explain racism's incredible power. Yet, as long as this illusion is maintained, the energy for change will be focused only on improving individual attitudes and actions, and the actual power of racism which is lodged in society's systems and institutions will be untouched.

Another illustration is the illusion that the victims of racism are responsible for their own plight. Racism's victims are blamed for their problems in many ways. In our nation's inner cities, people of color are blamed for the deteriorating condition of their housing, even though it began long before they came there and continued because of their forced overcrowding. They are blamed for their unemployment and underemployment, even though our economic system requires varying degrees of unemployment in order to maintain itself. Amazingly, this illusion is so successful that even the victims of racism often believe that their suffering is a product of their own failures. It is, therefore, a matter of great importance to them, as well as to us, to find ways of exposing the disguises and illusions that hide racism's power. We will be able to comprehend the definition of racism as prejudice plus power only to the degree that we are able to see this power at work.

One of the reasons we are fooled by such illusions is that most of us do not participate directly in the enforcing of our prejudices. We do not actually feel as though we are exercising the power that results in victimizing people of color. We do participate, however, even when this power is exercised for us by others in ways that are to our benefit.

Measured by Results

The validity of our definition of racism, prejudice plus power, depends in part on whether it is measurable. It is important that we have an effective and consistent means of measuring the presence, absence, and intensity of racism, as well as its increase or decrease over a period of time. The power of racism can be measured in three possible ways:

1. By judging a person's intentions. Whether racism exists in a given situation might be determined by whether or not those involved actually intend harm by their acts on the basis of race. This means of measuring racism is most often used by the criminal justice system, especially by the courts. While it may be useful in legal situations to determine individual guilt or innocence, it is not a valid means of measuring the presence or absence of racism. Indeed, racism is often perpetrated by people who have no racist intent. Thus, this means of measuring the power of racism has only limited usefulness.

2. By determining the amount and the extent of existing legislation to prohibit or control racism. The existence of laws that oppose racism is, of course, crucially important. The very fact that thirty years ago, racism was still protected by law, and today that situation is, for the most part, reversed, is a major sign of progress. However, one obvious problem is that the mere existence of a law does not guarantee that it will be implemented and enforced. Furthermore, as we have noted earlier, laws can be changed, as well as weakened, by the interpretation of the courts. A third and far more serious problem is that racism can circumvent the law, operating in increasingly subtle, sophisticated, and extralegal ways, always one step ahead of the law.

3. By measuring results—the only truly effective way. Simply stated, this means that significant deviations from the norm with regard to race in the statistical measuring of housing, education, employment, wages, and other factors of a community lead to the conclusion that racism is at work. Efforts to eliminate racism must be reflected in statistical change. For example, in the workplace, employment and wage gaps should narrow; in medical care, the statistical gap reflecting conditions of health should decrease.

To measure the conditions within a society and to explain deviations from the norm is, of course, a very complex process. For every statistical deviation there are many possible explanations, such as historical background, cultural variations, and differences in values. However, it is also possible to make statistical adjustments that take such factors into account. When this is done, it is possible to measure the results of racism with some degree of accuracy.

Summary

In this section, we have described the first component of our definition of racism, namely that racism is the power of one racial group in a society to impose its will upon and exploit another: prejudice plus power. Furthermore, racism can be disguised in order to create the illusion that it does not exist. The only effective means of measuring racism's power is by its results.

Racism Is a White Problem

If we define racism as prejudice plus power, the obvious question is, who's got the power? And the answer is equally obvious. In the United States, only one racial group has the power to impose its will upon and exploit other racial groups. Only one racial group has the power to pretend that racism does not exist. Therefore, in the United States, racism is a white problem, and only a white problem.

This conclusion will be traumatic for many readers of this book. The first difficulty is in the assertion that racism is only a white problem, that it is exclusively a disorder of white people and not of people of color. The second and most important difficulty is that if racism is a white problem, it changes dramatically the way we look at and attempt to solve it. Let us, to begin with, address several questions surrounding the issue of exclusiveness, and then come to the central issue.

Does this conclusion mean that racism in other parts of the world is only white racism? No, but in this book we are dealing only with racial justice issues in the United States. In other nations other racial groups may be dominant in the society and use their power to victimize others. Here, however, we are dealing with racism in the United States.

Does "white racism" mean that every white person is racist? Yes, every white person is part of the problem, but not necessarily with personal racist intent. We are assuming that most white Americans do not want to be racist. Every white person participates in and benefits from the system of racism, even if it is against our will.

Aren't many white people just as powerless as people of color? It is true that many white people face issues of powerlessness on other grounds than race. Because of racism, however, white skin is a benefit, a source of power and privilege, and nonwhite skin is a liability. What this definition recognizes is that the white society collectively imposes its power on people of color, and benefits from the exercise of that power. And it recognizes that the opposite is not true: none of the other racial groups in America have the collective power to control or dominate the white society or each other.

Does this mean that people of color are not racist? In the United States, people of color cannot be racist because they lack the power to enforce their prejudices. Many cannot even determine what happens in their own lives and communities, as the "big foot" analysis demonstrates. In all the efforts of past decades to bring about change and to resolve issues of racial injustice, there has been very little transfer of power. So long as power in America is distributed in an unequal and unjust manner, there can be no such thing as red racism, black racism, yellow or brown racism, or any form of "reverse racism." Racism in America is the exclusive property of the white community.

If not racism, what do we call the anger and hostility that people of color may direct toward whites, especially in the form of irrational and violent attacks on complete strangers? The answer to this is very important. To begin with, most people of color repress and internalize an enormous amount of anger—anger that may be expressed in ways that are destructive to themselves as individuals as well as to their own communities. This is one of the most demonic aspects of racism. A far more appropriate goal is for this anger to be directed against the system of white racism. At times (but not nearly as often as is projected by our white fears) this internalized rage is expressed in irrational and violent ways against white people. While violence in revenge is no more excusable than any other violence, such situations become even more complex when whites, protected by our system, refuse to examine the reasons that underlie unwarranted or arbitrary actions by people of color. Whatever the specific situation, the point here is that such negative behavior by people of color cannot be designated as racist because they lack the collective power to enforce their will.

The ironic twist here is that although there can be no "reverse racism" by people of color, it is, in fact, possible for people of color unwittingly and unwillingly to act the part of white racists. This means that their energies and actions can be used to support the system that oppresses them. In order to survive, they are trapped into helping to cause their own victimization. There are thousands of ways in which people of color are required to do this for the sake of their daily survival. We will be looking at many illustrations of this in the chapter on institutional racism.

What about tensions and conflict between and among African Americans, Asians, Native Americans, and Hispanics? This cannot be defined as racism, because these groups do not have the power to control one another. More often than not, such situations are direct results of white racism because these groups are often placed into competition with one another for living space and jobs. When this competition results in confrontation and conflict between communities of color, the media suggest that we are seeing intergroup racism. In reality we may be seeing another product of white racism.

Solving the Wrong Problem

Now to the central issue raised by the assertion that racism is a white problem. We have been trying to solve the wrong problem. For years, we have been trying to change the wrong people. With the best of intentions we were aiming in the wrong direction. Almost all of our nation's social and political initiatives for solving racial problems attempt to change the victims of racism and the conditions within their communities. In doing so, they avoid the real issue. Concerned people, in the firm belief that racial problems must be solved and racial conflicts reconciled, have devoted time, effort, and money to help Native Americans, Hispanics, Asians, and African Americans with their problems. The churches, the government, the universities, and many other groups work hard to help change people of color. Our assumption is that if we pour enough money into changing the victims of racism, they will catch up with us and will achieve a state of equality. But it isn't happening. And why? Because we are trying to change the wrong people.

The racial problem of the United States is not a minority problem. It is a majority problem. The cause is in the white society. The effects are felt in the communities of color. The problems of African Americans, Native Americans, Hispanics, and Asians are only the symptoms of European America's sickness. The white society owns the racial ghettos of America. We control them, maintain them, and condone them. What happens there is determined by the institutions and agencies of white America. All the programs in the world aimed at changing the victims of racism will ultimately be useless if those institutions and structures that create and control the conditions in the first place are not changed. This is very hard to accept for those of us who are white because our own happiness and lifestyle depend on these institutions and structures in their present form.

Remember the story of the Happiness Machine and the problem of its dross? No one has made us see that the forces responsible for the problems of people of color in our society are the same forces that sustain our own lives. No one has made us see that the condition of the minority of our citizens is a direct product of the majority's struggle for happiness. It is, therefore, not surprising that all our effort to solve the problems in our communities of color have caused so much frustration and met with so little success. We have tried to limit the effects of the dross without cutting off its flow. We have tried to help others to change without realizing that it requires change in ourselves.

It is not that people of color do not need or want to change. Just the opposite is true. However, we assume their problems are caused by the victims themselves rather than the institutions of the victimizers. And we assume that the cure for their illnesses begins with them and needs to be administered by us. And then, to add the final blow, the "cure" is administered by the very institutions that created the problem in the first place. It is as though an airplane were spraying poison gas over a city, causing the inhabitants to sicken and die. The owners of the airplane neither admit to the poisoning nor promise to stop. They do, however, sign a contract to develop an antidote for the gas. While the antidote is being developed, the gassing continues. When the antidote is ready, the pilots are directed to spray it, together with the poison gas, when they next fly over the city.

If we were to double or triple our efforts to bring about change for the victims of racism through increased housing, better education, more employment, and other social improvements, we might achieve some statistical progress. However, we would set two forces in the white society into even greater contradiction with each other: the one that creates and perpetuates inhuman conditions, and the one that tries to correct the results. Thus the sickness itself, which is not in the communities of color but in the white community, goes unchallenged because we are trying to change the wrong people. The name of this problem is white racism. And the only way to deal with it is by changing the systems and institutions of the United States that dominate, control, and exploit people of color for the benefit of whites. Simply changing attitudes is not enough. Helping the victims of racism is not enough. Only by reducing the power that enforces our prejudice will significant progress in dismantling white racism be made.

Is *Racism* Too Strong a Word?

One often hears the plea for a softer, more acceptable name for this problem. Why offend people with the personal accusation that is implied in *racism* and stated even more strongly in the phrase "white racism"? These concerns cannot be ignored. Although our definition, prejudice plus power, suggests a collective responsibility rather than personal guilt, the word *racism* still causes many people to react defensively. We need to find an approach to these issues that is liberating and less imprisoning.

However, there is another far more important reason for continuing to use the word *racism* and the phrase "white racism," and that is our tendency to evade the issue, to escape from reality. The history of our nation demonstrates the lengths to which we will go in order to avoid dealing with racism and its results. Our society has trouble admitting that racism exists. Even when such an admission is finally made, it is quickly dismissed and forgotten.

A powerful illustration of this tendency comes from the civil rights movement. The issue of white racism was forced into the open in 1968 by the National Advisory Commission on Civil Disorders, popularly known as the Kerner Commission. The Kerner Commission was appointed by President Lyndon Johnson to investigate the violence and revolt in the urban Black ghettos in the mid-sixties. The commission reported that the major cause of urban unrest was racism in the white society. Although it dealt directly with this subject in only a few sentences of its 600-page report, these few sentences caused a furor among white Americans:

> What white Americans have never fully understood—but what the Negro can never forget —is that the white society is deeply implicated in the ghetto. White institutions created it, white institutions maintain it and white society condones it. White racism is essentially responsible for the explosive mixture which has accumulated in our cities since the end of World War II.[3]

The response to this statement was something akin to the public exposure of a family scandal. Shock, anger, and denial came first. Then the matter was quickly hushed up, and the Kerner Commission's report was put on the shelf to be largely ignored. Even concerned liberals, who at first seemed willing to deal more openly with racism, soon agreed that open discussion of racism only produces negative reaction among whites and becomes counterproductive. Their suggested solution was to deal with other issues and use them to get at the problem of racism in a more indirect but safer and less offensive manner. However, each time such a solution is tested, the results are exactly as predicted. The issue of racism, or whatever softer name it is given, is forgotten as soon as it is put aside for other less threatening matters.

There is no soft, polite way to discuss the problem. The name by which it must be called is white racism. To call it anything else is to avoid the real issue, and there are few problems we try harder to avoid. No other less offensive designation is accurate. There is no way of approaching the subject indirectly. It is the unique problem of white America. It is white racism.

Summary

The first component of our definition was that racism is prejudice plus power. In this second component we have seen that the power of racism in the United States lies solely in the hands of the white society, and it is therefore an exclusively white problem. The changes most urgently required must be made in the white community. They are urgently required not only for people of color, but for our own sake as well.

Racism Is a White Prison

Now we have reached the heart of the matter. The third component of our definition of racism takes us to the central issue of this book: that we not only hold the power of racism in our hands, but that we are unable to let it go. We are prisoners of our own racism. In this section we shall explore the ways in which the power of racism, which hurts and destroys people of color, also hurts and destroys us as white people. We will also examine the biblical/theological concept of slavery and freedom. In order to introduce this part of our analysis, I would like to tell a story and share a personal experience.

"Go Home and Free Your Own People"

In the summer of 1967, a band of Black marchers, led by Stokely Carmichael, executive director of the Student Nonviolent Coordinating Committee (SNCC), carried out demonstrations across the state of Mississippi. The civil rights movement was still very strong, and this march could have been just another of the hundreds of marches and demonstrations taking place that summer. Yet it was a turning point. As the group marched, a new demand came in the form of a chant from the demonstrators, a controversial and insistent demand that had not been heard before. The chant and the demand were: Black power! Black power! Black power! The chant was quickly taken up by others, and the demand for Black power was repeated in towns and cities throughout the country. Thus, the Black power movement was born, and as a result the direction and strategies of the civil rights movement were significantly altered.

A direct result of the demand for Black power was a second demand that emerged during that summer of 1967. This second demand did not become as familiar to the public, but to its limited audience it was just as controversial and insistent as the demand for Black power. It was directed specifically at the relatively small number of white people like me who were living and working in Black communities throughout the South and in the northern cities of America. The demand was, "Whitey, go home and free your own people!" Just as the demand for Black power changed the direction of the civil rights movement, so also were the role and the perception of many white people altered by this second demand for us to "go home and free our own people."

Looking back to that moment in the summer of 1967 from the perspective of several decades later, I can identify the changes brought about by this demand as both redemptive and liberating. But it certainly did not feel that way to many of us at the time! At first we felt only rejection and confusion. We were shocked and angry. It took a long time before the tensions caused by this demand were resolved. These were not the usual tensions between Blacks and whites. We were not the Klan, or the White Citizens Council, or the police. We were those white people working the hardest for change. We were the white people holding hands with Blacks, and singing "Black and white together." We were the ones who had dedicated our lives to working in minority communities in the South and the urban ghettos of the north. And we felt that we were being told we were in the way, that we were not wanted. We were being forced out of the Black community, and we didn't like it. But the worst insult of all was that we were being identified with other white people, lumped together with those who were obviously racist. We felt hurt, angry, and rejected.

What we didn't realize until later is that we weren't being rejected. Rather, we were being pushed in the right direction—in a direction few of us would voluntarily have taken. The new direction was to work with white people and to work for change in the white community. For me personally, and for many others, it was the beginning of new discoveries. Being "lumped together with racists" was the best thing that could have happened to me. I began to understand for the first time my own identity as a racist. More important, I began to accept my identity as a white person and my identity with my own people. And I began to understand something about what change and liberation could mean to us. Some months later, I began for the first time to develop and implement education and training programs to help white people organize against racism in the white community.

Will Campbell, a southern preacher, writer, and civil rights organizer, tells how a similar experience changed his life and ministry. His "conversion" happened as he sat with friends, following the murder of a clergy colleague by a Klansman named Thomas Coleman. His realization: that the Thomas Colemans of the world are not the real enemy. They also are children of God, enslaved, loved, and in need of God's liberating word. Here are Campbell's words:

> Suddenly everything became clear. Everything. It was a revelation. . . . I was laughing at myself, at twenty years of a

ministry which had become, without my realizing it, a ministry of liberal sophistication . . . a theology of law and order and of denying not only the Faith I professed to hold but my history and my people—the Thomas Colemans. Loved. And if loved, forgiven. And if forgiven, reconciled. Yet sitting then in his own jail cell, the blood of two of his and my brothers on his hands.[4]

Racist and Not Free

"Go home and free your own people." Behind this admonition lies an assumption that is very strange to us and difficult to grasp. It is that white people, along with people of color, are not free. Racism is a prison for us too. In a sophisticated process of incorporation, every white person in America is willingly or unwillingly made a permanent participant in America's system of white racism. The major thesis that underlies the analysis of racism presented in this book is based on this assumption, that individually and corporately, we white Americans are enslaved in racism and need to be set free.

At one time, because of a we/they mentality, I thought it was possible to separate white Americans into two camps: the righteous and the racist. I, of course, was a member of the righteous camp. I assumed that the occupants of each camp were there by choice. I believed that my friends and I had wisely chosen to be nonracists, and those in the other camp had unwisely chosen to be racists. Now I know differently. I know there is no such thing as a nonracist camp. I know that, along with every other white American, I am a racist, and a member of the racist camp. I also know that most of us are not in this camp by choice. In many ways, we are prisoners in our own communities, prisoners of racism.

I never wanted to be a racist. I still don't. For a long time, I even thought I wasn't, but now I know I am. And I know how I got that way. Whenever I think about it, I become enraged and feel hurt deep inside myself. It is not guilt I feel—not anymore—just burning pain and anger over the fact that I was made into a racist. It happened to you too. Whether you like it or not, you were made into a racist. And you still are one. It should make you angry. Perhaps you share my rage, perhaps you don't. But I hope that by the time you finish reading this book, you will.

Strangely enough, being a racist does not necessarily mean being a terrible person. In all probability, you are not a conscious bigot who calls people "nigger" or who is unhappy about the prospect of freedom and justice for people of color. Nor are you intentionally responsible for the continued poverty, segregation, and powerlessness of people of color in America. If only it were as simple a problem as intentional racism! But our definition of racism, prejudice plus power, means that all of us who are white are part of and inseparable from a society that continually and systematically subordinates people of color. Whether or not we are intentional bigots, we are all locked inside a system of structured racism. As American citizens, every white person supports, benefits from, and is unable to be separated from white racism.

Nor is guilt the issue we are dealing with here. Unfortunately, many definitions of racism go no further than to make us feel guilty. They are based on the assumption that we are conscious and intentional racists who need continuously to feel guilty and confess the sin over and over again. If we are foolish enough to accept such definitions, we are automatically manipulated into responding in one of two ways. Either we deny the sin and waste time running around in defensive circles trying to prove our innocence. Or we admit our sin and waste time running around in charitable circles trying to pay off our guilt. Dealing with our racism does not mean allowing ourselves to become puppets controlled by our guilt-strings. The alternative to racism is freedom, not another kind of slavery. Too many people never get beyond the question of guilt. Guilt is among the most ineffective motivations for positive human action. The only purpose of guilt, according to Christian teaching, is to drive us to seek forgiveness. The guilt-laden person just wallows in guilt. The forgiven person is freed to act.

Of course, repentance and confession are crucially important in combating racism. Conscious and overt racists should feel guilty. They need to repent and seek forgiveness. And each of us needs to continue to examine ourselves and discover, confess, and eliminate the prejudice and bigotry that are still a part of our attitudes, thoughts, and actions. Moreover, our nation as a whole needs still to come to repentence for its racism. Jim Wallis, editor of the magazine *Sojourner,* calls racism "America's original sin." He also writes that "white America has yet to realize the extent of its racism . . . much less to repent of its racial sins."[5]

Confessing our sin is only the first step, however. When we have been forgiven, our guilt has been dealt with. We have been empowered to go beyond guilt to the next step, which is to face our unwitting and unwilling imprisonment in racism, which *continues even after we have repented, confessed, and been forgiven.* As white Americans, we are racist oppressors, even when we don't want to be. Against our own conscious wills, each of us participates in the corporate acts of a society that victimizes its minority people. Without conscious awareness of decision, we were made into persons whose thoughts, feelings, values, and actions are racist. As white oppressors we are ourselves oppressed. The imprisoner is imprisoned, the victimizer victimized. We are prisoners in the racist structures of American society, and we need to be set free. C. Eric Lincoln describes this imprisonment of the imprisoner: "The same fetters that bind the captive bind the captor, and the American people are captive of their own myths, woven so clearly and so imperceptively into the fabric of our national experience."[6]

In our white American mentality nothing could be more abrasive to us than the idea that we are not free. As Americans we sing, speak, and pray about ourselves as people who are already free, whose freedom is already attained and needs only to be preserved with diligence and shared with missionary zeal. We are the people who fought off colonial oppression and gained our independence. Our country is called the land of the free and the home of the brave. We give thanks to God at least every Fourth of July and Thanksgiving Day that we are a free people and that we no longer have to struggle for our freedom like most other people in the world.

This belief that we are already free has been the determining factor in setting our goals for resolving racial conflicts. We begin with the assumption that people of color need and want to become free like us. We want to help them "come up to our level." When we speak of equality, we mean we want them to become equal to us. All of these goals proclaim that we do not need to change, or become free ourselves. We have difficulty believing that we, too, as well as people of color, are oppressed and need liberation.

It is at this point that the teachings of the Christian faith come into direct confrontation with popular American religious beliefs that often pass themselves off as Christianity. The Christian faith teaches that all people are broken, oppressed, and enslaved, and that all people need freedom, salvation, and redemption, and that these needs enter into every aspect of a person's life. By contrast, in popular American religion, rather than being defined as a passionately felt need, a desperate hope, or an exciting surprise, salvation is defined only as a "spiritual" aspect of one's life and is usually taken for granted. The desire for redemption has been replaced by an arrogant defense of our present way of life. And, since freedom is defined solely in political rather than theological terms, the last thing that popular American religion will accept is the idea that white, middle-class Americans are oppressed or enslaved, either by racism or by any other power.

Slaves to Sin, Freed by Grace

Further light can be shed on this conflict between Christianity and popular American religion by turning to the Bible. When Jesus preached his first sermon, he announced the purpose of his ministry by quoting from the prophet Isaiah:

> "The Spirit of the Lord is upon me,
>   because he has anointed me to bring good news to the
>   poor.
>   He has sent me to proclaim release to the captives
>   and recovery of sight to the blind,
>   to let the oppressed go free,
>   to proclaim the year of the Lord's favor." (Luke 4:18-19)

The gospel of Jesus Christ has always been and is today a means of freedom only for enslaved people, a means of healing only for people who are sick. Jesus lived and died for the sake of the downtrodden, the poverty-stricken, the suffering, the sick, and the dying—all who were then and are now oppressed. Not only the ministry of Jesus, but the actions of God throughout history, as recorded in the Old and New Testaments, were almost always reported in terms of liberating oppressed people. Moses was sent to free the Hebrew people from enslavement in Egypt. Isaiah proclaimed comfort and release to the captives of Babylon. The prophets were sent to demand justice for the poor who were being oppressed by rich countrymen. The Psalmist prayed for rescue from his enemies and tormenters. St. Paul and the early Christians discovered and celebrated their liberation from the law, from sin, death, and the devil. And when they were harassed, imprisoned, and killed by their Roman rulers, they looked forward to their ultimate liberation in the new Jerusalem.

The Christian message has not changed. It is the same today as it always has been. It is a gospel of liberation for oppressed people. It is good news to the poverty-stricken in the ghettos of our land. It is the proclamation of liberty to the captives in our prisons and on our reservations. It is sight for the blind, strength for the lame, community for the lonely. It is freedom for the oppressed people of the United States and the world. And—this must be doubly emphasized—*this is all the gospel there is!* There are not two gospels, one for those who are down and out, and one for those who are up and about. There is not one Christianity for those who need freedom, and another Christianity for those who don't. There is one gospel of Jesus Christ. It is the gospel of liberation offered to all those who identify themselves as oppressed.

This does not mean, however, that the gospel is only for the poor and for people of color. It is also for the middle class and for white people. When we hear that Jesus came only to heal the sick, make whole the broken ones, and free the captive, it is amazing how we so often assume that this does not refer to us. Yet, when Jesus dealt with the upstanding, righteous, educated, religious upper-class people of his day, his main goal was to help them understand their sickness, their brokenness, and their enslavement. For this was the only way he could bring healing, wholeness, and freedom to them also. When he confronted the Pharisees, he tried to make them see their slavery. When he addressed the rich young ruler, as well as others from the upper classes or from the military, it was on the basis of the need that Jesus knew they had for healing and wholeness. It was for the sake of these people that he said the words, "It is not the healthy who need a doctor," and "I have not come to call the righteous, but sinners." Those on the underside of society do not need to be informed of their status.

There cannot be two versions of Christianity, one for the poor and one for the rich, one gospel for white people and another for people of color. There is only one gospel, and that is the one that brings liberation for the oppressed. White, middle-class people need to be liberated as much as anyone else. If you and I are ready to consider ourselves as oppressed people, then the gospel is for us too.

False Division: Oppressor and Oppressed

It may seem ironic at first that because of our role as oppressors, our identity is exposed as oppressed people in need of liberation. But from the point of view of the Bible, it is not ironic but quite natural. The truth is that we would not be racists if we were not oppressed and imprisoned by the forces of sin and evil. It is because we are imprisoned by much larger forces of evil that we cannot prevent ourselves from being used to oppress others. For this reason Dr. Al Pero, a Lutheran African American theologian, challenges the theological position that divides the world into oppressor and oppressed. The following words are from notes of a lecture by Dr. Pero:

> You simply cannot be true to the Bible and divide the world into oppressors and oppressed. Of course, it is true that the rich and the powerful of the world have created systems that oppress the poor. And, of course, we have to organize to try to stop them. But we also have to try to change them while we're trying to stop them. Likewise, there are a lot of poor people who are so busy oppressing their own sisters and brothers that they haven't found out what liberation is yet either. We have to help change them, too. The Bible does not proclaim that all the rich people are going to hell because they are oppressors, while all the poor people are going to automatically go to heaven because they are oppressed. But

it does say that God's liberation is for both of these groups of people. If you're going to divide the world into two categories on the basis of what the Bible says, the division has to be between those who are aware that they are oppressed and those who are not aware that they are oppressed. You just can't come along with any other conclusions and call yourself a Christian theologian or a liberation theologian or any other kind of theologian.

The Bible and the church have been teaching this for centuries. But we have just forgotten about it and pretended these teachings were never given to us. They have been teaching that the oppressors are just as oppressed as the oppressed, and if that weren't so, they wouldn't be going around oppressing people. So if you're going to have a theology that looks at the rich and powerful through the Bible's eyes, you're going to have to say that they do these ridiculous and stupid things because they are oppressed by sin and are in need of liberation.[7]

Enslaved by sin and freed by grace: this is the biblical message to all people, to people of color and white people alike. True, each group's experiences of enslavement are quite different, but the promise of grace applies equally to both. And the new life in grace must be a life together in which free people from all communities struggle together for a just future.

There is one other major difference in applying this formula of "slave to sin and free by grace" to each racial community. Since we in the white community have far greater difficulty in recognizing our enslavement to racism, the odds of our reaching out for grace are significantly reduced. Therefore the urgency is even greater that new efforts to combat racism be implemented, especially since the community of color is also so greatly affected by whether white people change.

There's bad news and good news in the phrase, "Whitey, go home and free your own people." It means that we are not free; that's the bad news. But our being sent on this "mission to white people" is a sign of hope that our people can be free, and that's the good news. It is the good news of the gospel that although we are enslaved by sin, we can be freed by grace. Our mission to white people is to carry this news to our white sisters and brothers. Our mission, as symbolized by the fable in chapter one, is to help write an ending to the story which will be for the benefit of all.

Summary

In this chapter we have presented and explored three components of a definition of racism: first, racism is prejudice plus power; second, the power of racism in the United States is exclusively in the hands of the white society; and third, the power of racism imprisons and enslaves white people as well as people of color. The goal of overcoming racism is for the sake of all. The Bible and the historic teachings of the Christian faith offer freedom to the enslaved and liberation for the oppressed. This is all the gospel there is, and it is this gospel that offers hope and direction for combating racism and building a multicultural church and society.

3

INDIVIDUAL RACISM

To be white in America is
not to have to think about it.
—Robert Terry

Racism, then, creates two prisons, not just one. The first is the prison of oppressed people of color in America, the miserably uncomfortable, poverty-haunted ghetto. The inmates are African American and Hispanic people in the inner cities and rural areas of the United States, Native Americans confined on reservations, Asians in crowded "Chinatowns." Unless we have been totally deaf and blind during these past decades of social turmoil and racial conflict, we are at least aware of this prison's existence, though we may be unclear about the reality and its implications.

The Comfortable Prison

The other prison created by racism is for us, the white people of America. Although we are in a prison we don't believe it, for our prison is deceptively comfortable and disarmingly warm and friendly. But it is a prison, nonetheless. You and I are its inmates, and it exists wherever we live, learn, work, and play. The walls of this prison are the residential, cultural, and institutional boundaries of white America. Its bars may be less visible, but they evoke as much frustration, loneliness, fear, and anxiety as the bars of any penitentiary.

The inmates of this other prison have a desperate need to pretend that it does not exist. An intricate web of deception disguises its reality. The bars on the windows are hidden by expensive curtains. There is thick carpeting instead of institutional flooring. Flowers and vines hide the steel plate doors. In place of a meager cot, there is a luxurious bed. The disguise is complete; the lie is convincing. The inmates live in the firm belief that there is no prison; that they exist in total freedom. Whenever we become aware of the confining and dehumanizing walls that surround us, we are quickly assured that they are the outside walls of the other prison—the prison for people of color—not our own.

This comfortable prison is ruled by racism in its three interlocking forms: individual, institutional, and cultural. In this chapter, we will examine how the first of the three, individual racism, is systematically produced and perpetuated in white Americans. We will describe how individual racists are created, and how we can begin the task of dismantling and undoing our individual racism. We will also take special care to distinguish individual racism from racism in its institutional and cultural expressions, and at the same time to identify the linkages among the three. For, as we shall see, individual racism could not exist without the others.

The Making of a Racist

Racists are made, not born. As we said earlier, all of us are born with a natural propensity for prejudice, and are taught the biases and prejudices of our families and peers. But we are not born racist. Remember our definition of racism: prejudice plus power. An individual's personal racial prejudices are transformed into racism by becoming linked to the power of societal systems. Without this linkage there could be no racism, and without the empowerment of systemic racism there could be no individual racists. Because of this linkage, however, an individual person whose prejudices might otherwise be limited to hurtful and ugly behavior in his or her private encounters becomes a violent and distructive instrument with far greater scope.

The linkage is automatic. As white individuals we unavoidably participate in a system that gives us power and privilege based on our racial identity. But our willing cooperation with this system is not automatic. Our active or passive acceptance of power and privilege requires a thorough process of socialization and conditioning. It begins early in our lives and continues throughout our childhood. By the time we are adults, our indoctrination is complete. The only escape is through a conscious decision to reject our right to this power and privilege and to participate in the struggle to dismantle the prison of racism.

How does this conditioning take place? How do we become so completely imprisoned that most of us are not aware of it, do not feel its restrictions and limitations? In the next few pages, we will examine four powerful forces that are brought to bear on every white individual, each of which contributes to this imprisonment.

Isolation

The prison of white racism is maintained by keeping its inmates separate from and unaware of people of color and the world in which they live. Legal segregation created two ghettos, not one. Just as most people of color were isolated from us, so also were most of us isolated from them. Even if, from within our white communities, we became aware of African Americans, Native Americans, Hispanics, and Asians, they were somewhere out there, in another part of town or in another part of the country. We seldom experienced their reality. Everything we knew about them was secondhand information and filled with distortions.

Twenty-five years after the end of legal segregation, we are still a nation that lives racially apart. It is true that information about other racial groups now flows more readily. We know more about each other. We may have a friend or two of another race or culture. But, for the vast majority of us, that is as far as it goes. We may think there is more contact between whites and people of color than there was in the past. Don't we attend school together, work together, and play together? In fact, we do not actually do these things together; we do them in the same place and in each other's presence, but we still do them separately. In desegregated schools, workplaces, and recreation areas, a strict, but informal segregation still exists. True integration in such groups is relatively rare. And, as soon as school, work, or play is completed, whites and people of color still go home to their segregated communities knowing, for the most part, little or nothing of each others' lives.

One of the most familiar symbols of our isolation and separation is a suburban home. It is touted by the advertising world as an escape—the fulfillment of a person's dreams. But its distance from the city, at the end of a freeway, surrounded by six-foot fences, makes it seem in many ways more like a prison than an escape. The English author and theologian C. S. Lewis, in his book *The Great Divorce*, described a vision of hell as a place where people perpetually move away from one another because of their inability to get along with each other. They leave houses and entire blocks and neighborhoods empty and build new houses at the edge of hell, thereby creating an ever-expanding circle with houses at the edge, and with the abandoned center left behind them.[1] Lewis's description of hell could be a description of white flight from the city after World War II and the emergence of suburbs in the United States. The development of suburbs not only created a great gulf between suburban whites and people of color in the inner cities; it also led to a sense of great isolation for many suburbanites. Anyone who has spent several hours every day on the freeway or commuter train understands the need for tranquilizers and alcohol in order to survive and still insist with a smile, "It really isn't so bad."

Anesthesia

Anesthesia is the word used here to describe a second powerful force that conditions us to accept our imprisonment. I first became aware of this phenomenon from an African American woman. She attended an interracial seminar, and became angry at white participants for being on a "head trip," that is, for staying on intellectual levels and not getting involved with their feelings. She said something like this.

> You people really don't give a damn! But it's not that you don't want to. You just don't know how to. You don't know how to feel! Your heads have been cut off from your guts, and you've lost touch with your own feelings. Sure, you can empathize with the feelings of others, with the pain of other people's oppression, but you can't feel the pain of your own oppression and brokenness. You have been anesthetized to the agony of the destruction inside yourselves. If you could see and feel the effects of racism on your own people, you would not be able to tolerate it. You would not be able to control your anger. There would be a white rage in your community that would make Black rage seem cool. But you white people have lost your ability to feel. The best you can do is understand with your minds, with no response from your emotions.

Anesthesiologists prescribe drugs to reduce or eliminate pain during surgery and convalescence. From aspirin to morphine, from slight loss of sensation to total unconsciousness, the medical profession can seal us off from our feelings. On a psychological level also, an anesthetizing process takes place when a person becomes trapped in painful human predicaments from which there seem to be no escape. Slum dwellers, for example, become less and less aware of their crowded conditions and of the debris and waste that surround them. Prison inmates anesthetize themselves into indifference to the claustrophobic effects of their confinement. Soldiers on patrol learn to prevent the fear of ambush from driving them insane. Unhappily married partners who no longer work at the marriage seal themselves off from each other's hostility. Anesthesia can be useful when a person is hopelessly and unalterably in pain. But it can also be evil by concealing reality; by encouraging the pretense that the pain is not real and, therefore, that there is no need to diagnose the cause. Throughout history, when tyrants have sought to enslave fellow human beings, a primary technique has been to anesthetize them to the effects of their bondage by removing their hope of ever returning to freedom.

People of color in America recognize that this process is used as a weapon against them. They see it in the false promises of the politicians. They see it in the escapist reassurances of pacifying religion disguised as Christianity. They see it in the oblivion of drugs available on every city street corner and in the deadening effects of alcohol on every Indian reservation. Whatever form the anesthesia takes, it results in the same repression of legitimate anger. Only when the rage builds up beyond even the anesthetic's power to prevent its expression, does one see the depth of the hurt and pain as it explodes in uncontrollable and irrational behavior. Numerous studies demonstrate a link between the internalized anger and repressed rage that results from racial injustice and the excessive violence and crime in communities of color.[2]

Anesthesia is also used against white people to deaden our feelings in the comfortable prison. The most severe marks of our conditioned racism are not the bigotry and fear that have been brainwashed into us. Rather, they are the placid acceptance of our ghettoized condition, and the permission implied by our silence and nonresistance to continued segregation from reality. The anesthetizing forces make it possible for us to go about our normal lives as though we were not being held in bondage; as though there were no alternatives to our present way of life. Robert Terry, an analyst and educator on racism and racial justice, puts it succinctly: "To be white in America," he says, "is not to have to think about it."[3]

Germany: A Personal Witness

In Germany, more than thirty years ago, I discovered how this socializing anesthesia, accompanied by layers of insulation, works to isolate us from reality. In 1960, I was a graduate student at a German university. There, my consciousness was first awakened to the reality of racism in America.

Before and during World War II, the National Socialists (or Nazis) had carried out the extermination of more than six million Jews. After the facts of this holocaust became known, the majority of Germans insisted that they didn't know it was happening. In response to these denials the entire world asked incredulously, "How can it be that you did not know?" I asked the same question of my German acquaintances and friends. With arrogance and self-righteousness, I challenged the assertion that they did not know about the persecution of the Jews that was happening before their very eyes.

Then, toward the end of my studies I participated in a seminar at the German Evangelical Academy on the subject, "Race Relations Around the World." There I was introduced to the reality of race relations in the United States, described in graphic historical and contemporary detail. It was the time of the civil rights movement when the push to desegregate schools and public accommodations in the South was causing major upheavals, such as the events at Little Rock, Arkansas. I was embarrassed to admit to my German colleagues that I knew virtually nothing about current racial realities in America. Most shocking, however, was an estimate by one of the speakers that the number of people of color who had been killed by white people in America since the time of Columbus was approximately six million, the same number as that of Jews who had been killed in the Holocaust! And I heard myself say the same words as the Germans: "I didn't know." And indeed, it had been hidden from me, and I was honestly not aware of it, at least on a conscious level. I had found the answer to why the Germans could say, "We didn't know it was happening."

Privileges and Rewards

Even though we are using imagery of involuntary conditioning and imprisonment, each of us has participated to a great degree in our own deception. This is nowhere more evident than in our willingness to accept the rewards and benefits, the payoffs of racism. As we grow older, we accept privileges, comforts, and often riches that come to us almost automatically as white middle- and upper-class Americans. We join in the pretense that we earn these privileges through our own efforts, initiative, and superior intelligence. We do not acknowledge that these gifts really fall into our laps; nor do we often admit that those who do not share the benefits are as deserving as we. We need to be honest with ourselves.

Often we remain under the control of our jailers because we wish to protect the benefits we have "worked so hard" to achieve. Bluntly put, it is our greed that keeps us attached to our chains, loyal to the warden of the prison.

What are these rewards and privileges? They are all around us, seemingly nameless and countless. But it is important that we begin naming and counting them. There are, of course, the rewards of better and more accessible education and jobs, and the benefits of higher salaries. And there are our better living conditions, our better health and health care, and many other large-scale rewards.

But there are also the smaller, day-to-day privileges that are so easily accepted and taken for granted. A list of these "white skin privileges," in comparison with people of color, might begin with the ease that we have in cashing a check, in walking without suspicion in a department store, or in having our contribution recognized in a discussion. The list could continue with the central place white people have in our history books, the image of white people compared with people of color in the media, or our power as white people in determining values and ethics in public life. Because of white skin privilege, we can also be confident that our racial identity will not be used against us in applying for a job, looking for a house, relating to public authorities, or using public accommodations. This list can go on and on. Readers need to develop their own lists and become conscious of their own rewards and benefits for white skin privilege.

At the same time, we must be absolutely clear that these privileges and rewards come to us automatically, whether we ask for them or not, whether we agree with having them or not. The very same institutions that are responsible for our socialization into racist beliefs and values also create and bestow the advantages of white skin privileges. Not only do they come to us automatically, but the socialization process make us oblivious to their existence. Even when we are directly confronted with the reality of racism's rewards, our first instinct is not to believe in their existence and especially to deny our possession of them.

The purpose of becoming aware of these privileges and rewards is not to make us feel bad, but to become more aware of that which we are struggling to change. As we shall see more clearly in the next chapter, the systems and institutions that bestow and control these privileges must be changed, and not simply our individual desire to receive them.

Our own awareness begins, however, not only with the realization of our imprisonment in racism, but also by realizing the purpose of these rewards, which is to keep us uncomplaining about our bonds. Only when we realize that our losses are far more than our benefits will we join fully in the effort to transform the institutions that both imprison and reward us. Robert Terry addresses this clearly:

> The better we are at pinpointing the losses of racism and highlighting the advantages of moving beyond those losses, the greater are our chances of dealing with the causes rather than the symptoms of racism.[4]

Programming and Conditioning

In April 1968, shortly after the assassination of Dr. Martin Luther King Jr., Jane Elliot, a school teacher in Riceville, Iowa, led her all-white third grade class in a two-day experiment. She separated the blue-eyed children from the brown-eyed children. On the first day she taught them that blue-eyed children were superior to brown-eyed children and instituted rules that gave the blue-eyed children more power and privileges than the brown-eyed children. The results were almost immediate and overwhelming. The blue-eyed students delighted in their new status, and adapted easily to a role of superiority and dominance. The brown-eyed students were docile in adapting to their new and inferior identity and subjugated role, accepting their new station in life with little resistance and behaving accordingly. Even their test scores took an immediate plunge. The next day, the roles were reversed. So also, and instantly, were the behavior patterns. This experiment has been repeated with both children and adults many times since 1968. Each time, it demonstrates how susceptible human beings are to indoctrination into superior and inferior roles. This is a true story that was recorded on film, and is widely used in antiracism education programs.[5]

This story illustrates how vulnerable human beings are to such conditioning. In a society that is isolated, unaware, and anesthetized into believing that the prison does not exist, making racists out of each of us is a relatively simple task. From earliest childhood each of us goes through a subtle (and sometimes, not so subtle) socializing process. Consciously and unconsciously, intellectually and emotionally, a racist mentality has been created in each of us. We are taught to respond to the stimulus of whiteness with pride and identity, a sense of ease and respect. To the stimulus of what is perceived by whites to be African American, Hispanic, Native American, and Asian we are taught to respond with fear and hate, suspicion, paternalistic concern, and pity. So deeply are these responses embedded in us that no matter how much we reject them, they still control our lives. The very core of our being is permeated with racist assumptions and values. Surrounding that core are many layers of insulation that muffle our feeling, our vision, and our memory, making racism appear to be subtle, elusive, and difficult to perceive. Most of this conditioning takes place before we are old enough to understand. If we knew what was happening, some of us might object and rebel. But how could we know at such an early age that growing up in an almost totally white environment is a forced and unnatural existence in a country that has a large population of people of color? How could we know that the values passed on to us are based on the fact of white control and the unspoken assumption of white superiority? How could we know that what we learn about the achievements of white people and the failures of people of color is twisted and untruthful? In our isolated and carefully protected white environment, we have no opportunity to doubt, let alone challenge the orientation to life that we were given. White power, white control, and white superiority are presented to us as natural, the way things are and the way things ought to be.

Myths and Lies

An enormous list of myths and lies about people of color has been created to control the impressions and perceptions of whites as they relate to people of color. These myths and lies have been handed down from generation to generation of white people. The actual myths and lies vary from one generation to another. Basically, however, they come in two kinds of packages. The first contains the lies in their most blatant and crude forms. The second contains a more subtle and sophisticated version of the same myths and lies. Years ago, the blatant lies were generally believed by all white people. Even today, a significant portion of white Americans still maintains them. Such crude myths and lies simply declare that Americans of African descent are inferior, ugly, violent, dirty, oversexed animals. They are also happy, lazy, dancing, singing, stupid idiots. Native Americans are sneaky, lying, drunken, savage, pagan murderers. Hispanics are cheating, sleepy, ignorant, greasy, conniving thieves. Asians are slant-eyed, mysterious and inscrutable, untrustworthy, backstabbing gooks.

Those who accept these lies believe them to be fundamental truths. Most older readers will recognize them. Such perceptions were passed along through songs, jokes, movies, radio, and television. Are you old enough to remember Amos and Andy, Aunt Jemima, the Lone Ranger and loyal Tonto, the Cisco Kid and stupid Pancho? What about Stepin Fetchit or those good old Stephen Foster songs and minstrel shows? How about cowboy and Indian movies? Has ever before a nation celebrated the genocide of an indigenous people with such joy and pride? How could we be anything but callous in our feelings toward Native Americans when each time we saw a movie or turned on the television, John Wayne and his compatriots were wiping out another horde of red savages so that America could belong to the civilized white man?

To this day, such racist indoctrination influences our daily language and cultural symbols. To us, the color black symbolizes evil, sin, death; white stands for purity, virtue, and joy. Good guys wear white hats and ride white horses; bad guys wear black hats and ride black horses. Even today, "there's a nigger in a woodpile," there's a "nigger toe" in the nut tray, and one still hears the children's chant: "eenie, meenie, meinie, moe, catch a nigger by the toe."

Perhaps most devastating and demeaning of all: the still-prevailing sex mythology. "They all just want to get our women into bed!" More than any of such lies, it reveals our own insecurity and the need to project our own problems onto others. The projection of sexual stereotypes onto people of color, and especially onto African American men, our paranoia about Black men's desire for white women, coupled with the historical reality of the rape of Black women by white men, the castration and lynching of Black men, all still fester. One could almost believe that if the sexual insecurity of white males could be magically overcome, a large part of our white racism would also be ended.

A Kinder, Gentler Lie

The myths and lies in the second package are more subtle and sophisticated. They are designed for the post-civil rights movement generation. This new generation considers words such as "nigger" obscene, and has been taught to overcome its more blatant prejudices, as well as to be kind and respectful to people of color.

In this new situation, variations of the myths and lies are required. Although they are still perpetuated at all levels of white society today, they tend to assume a more sophisticated form, and are more acceptably packaged in academic concepts and language. No matter how it is stated, however, the white community still accepts the basic message that people of color are intellectually inferior, responsible for their own oppressed condition, deserving of our fear, mistrust, and occasional charity, and to be avoided in more than token numbers.

The ways in which these myths and lies are communicated by the media has also changed. Aunt Jemima and Tonto have been replaced by new images of successful, well-educated professionals who are in most ways just like you and me. They have the same joys and the same heartaches, the same strengths and the same foibles. They are one of us. Like us, they do not suffer from poverty, injustice, or inequality. And, most importantly, they are not presented as victims of racism, as people subject to the constant, never-ending penalty for being Black in "white America." They are false images created by the media that perpetuate today's myths and lies and prevent us from understanding the realities with which most people of color live. In a recent study of race and racial politics, *Racial Formation in the United States*, Michael Omi and Howard Winant assert that these myths and lies are so tightly woven into the fabric of our culture that they are virtually impossible to remove:

> The continuing persistence of racial ideology suggests that these racial myths and stereotypes cannot be exposed as such in the popular imagination. They are, we think, too essential, too integral, to the maintenance of the U.S. social order. Of course, particular meanings, stereotypes and myths can change, but the presence of a system of racial meanings and stereotypes, of racial ideology, seems to be a permanent feature of U.S. culture.[6]

White Lies

Alongside the lies about people of color, there are many lies about ourselves that have an even greater effect on our racism. And we find them so attractive to believe! However easy we may find it to accept the negative stereotypes of inferiority regarding people of color, it is even more seductive to believe that the opposing positive and superior qualities belong to us, the white people of America.

For centuries, we have been taught that our European American forebears demonstrated great physical and mental strength and superiority in winning American independence, taming the wild frontier, overcoming odds as immigrants, and, through that most admirable of all qualities, private initiative, amassing great fortunes and building a great economy. All of this is generally presented in stark contrast to the lesser achievements of people of color, and is laid before us as the standard of achievement for white Americans.

Add to these myths the liberal lies about our generosity, philanthropy, and willingness to share our freedom. We believe in nothing more strongly than our ideology of charity toward the poor and needy, without comprehending that charity is a poor substitute for justice, and that the ultimate consequence of charity without justice is to anesthetize giver and receiver alike.

Summary

Thus far in this chapter we have explored how individual white racists are created. White society is imprisoned in a system of racism that ghettoizes us as well as people of color. Individual persons are incorporated into the powerful system of white racism in four ways: through isolation, anesthetization, white privilege, and conditioning education. In our own comfortable prison, both blatant and subtle myths and lies about people of color and about ourselves are perpetuated and believed. Now we move on to explore how individuals become free of their racism.

Freedom for Individual Racists

A person in prison asks two burning questions. The first is "How do I survive here?" The second, "How do I get out?" Both are appropriate for persons like us, trapped in the prison of racism. The answers suggested here are presented as two dimensions of freedom. The first dimension speaks to the question of survival inside a prison. It is a declaration that true freedom cannot be taken from us; that it is possible to be free, even inside a prison. The second dimension is presented as an invitation to join a large and growing number of prisoners who are developing plans to break out of racism's prison. Complete freedom cannot come to an individual who tries to escape from racism's prison alone. Despite our images of famous individual prison breaks, true freedom comes from a prison break that frees all the prisoners and, in the process, destroys the prison. Our discussion begins with the first dimension.

Inside a prison's walls, behind bars, in solitary confinement, bound by chains, desperately sick, at the edge of death, it is possible to hold onto one's freedom. The enslaving power of an unjust state can imprison a person physically, even take away one's life. But, as a great many prisoners through the centuries have demonstrated, they do not have the power to take away a person's essential humanity and freedom.

The witnesses to this truth abound. St. Paul's great dissertations on freedom were written from a jail cell. Mahatma Ghandi and Martin Luther King Jr. taught and demonstrated that being in prison can even be a means of promoting freedom. Nelson Mandela, after twenty-seven years in prison, emerged to demonstrate that his identity as a free person had been strengthened in prison. And, during 300 years of enslavement, Africans in the United States never lost sight of freedom, and proclaimed in their spirituals that their slavemasters could "kill the body but not the soul."

This amazing reality applies equally to our imprisonment as white people within the system of racism. It is possible to be a free person, though still restricted within the prison walls of racism. It is possible to break the shackles of lies, no longer to be deceived, no longer to believe in or trust the lies, no longer to be controlled by anesthetizing and brainwashing. To become free of individual racism while still inside racism's prison is not a private activity, although it is an intensely personal one. It is an interpersonal process that calls for the building of community inside the prison, a community that supports and strengthens each person even when in solitary confinement, a community of fellow prisoners committed to the struggle against racism.

Understanding freedom for white people within the walls of racism's prison requires a clear distinction between the terms "nonracist" and "antiracist." Nonracists try to deny that the prison exists. Antiracists work for the prison's eventual destruction. So long as the prison exists, we are all inside. There can be no such thing as a nonracist, and it is a waste of time trying to become one. Trying to be seen as a nonracist by others is just another way of being racist. There can only be antiracists, who are free people inside the prison, working for the prison's ultimate destruction, working toward the elimination of racism in people and institutions. Robert Terry puts it this way:

> I am not personally offended when someone says being white in America makes me a white racist. That is true. I am offended, however, if someone says that is all I am. That is not true. I am both a racist and an antiracist, and, as an anti-racist, strongly committed to the elimination of racism.[7]

Becoming freed of individual racism, then, does not mean becoming a nonracist. In this sense, there are still great limitations to our freedom within the walls. However, it is possible to be simultaneously a racist and an antiracist. It is possible to be an unwilling, uncooperative prisoner, straining against the chains, refusing any longer to be anesthetized against the pain of imprisonment, and working to rid one's self of the countless effects of racist programming in a lifelong step-by-step process.

Being an antiracist means taking responsibility for one's own racism. Even though we know that our individual racism was imposed on us through conditioning and brainwashing, each of us ultimately shares responsibility for our continuing deception, and each of us is accountable for our freedom. Being an antiracist means, especially, rejecting the rewards and benefits that entice us to accept our confinement. This is perhaps the most difficult part of becoming free. We described earlier how greed keeps us enchained and loyal to the prison warden. We will be successful in rejecting our privileges only when we are convinced that the gains of freedom will far exceed the rewards of our comfortable prison.

Feeling Pain Again

Strange as it may seem, recovering from individual racism means welcoming the opportunity to feel pain. We must be willing to give up the anesthesia that deadens our nerves and prevents us from feeling the reality of our prison. We must submit to a process through which we will learn what has been done to us. When we are more able to feel, we will experience the pain of imprisonment, perhaps to the point of outrage. We will become aware of the ways in which racism hurts and destroys us, and how it uses us to hurt and destroy others. We will no longer be able to tolerate our own racism. We must tear down our curtains so that we can see and feel the prison bars. We must clearly understand that our comforts are no more than bribes, rewards for not insisting on our freedom. The comfortable prison with all its subtle means of oppression must be exposed for the destructive and evil instrument it is.

By ridding ourselves of the anesthesia, we will also be able to break down the debilitating power of guilt. Instead of guilt and defensiveness, we will begin to feel anger. For how else should we respond to a system that manipulates our lives, teaches us to hate, and makes us hated, a system that betrays us and lures us into prejudice, bigotry, and fear, and, as the crowning blow, makes us feel guilty and responsible. Guilt is debilitating, but anger has the power to break chains. When we realize that our racist system is a prison in which we, too, are locked, we will stop feeling guilty and use our anger to plot ways of breaking out. In an article entitled "Rage and Reconciliation," Catherine Meeks from Mercer University writes this:

> White people as well as black people have a responsibility to be honest about their rage. White people have plenty of rage which demands acknowledgment, as well as guilt about the heritage of slavery . . .
>
> Yes, there is rage in you and in me, too. It's OK. It's real. God loves us in spite of it. It doesn't matter how we feel. The good news is that as we own our rage it can become a thing which we can control instead of letting it control us. As we move into our journeys toward wholeness and allow the light of Calvary to shine upon us, that rage can be transformed into energy which heals instead of destroys.[8]

An important part of our de-anesthetization occurs as we recall the past and try to discover in our personal histories how we were made into racists. We will also need to reexamine the history of the United States, and how its distortions are part of the system's conspiracy to fill us with racist myths and lies. For those of us who hold the Christian faith as the center of our lives, the first step in such a process is to remember our baptism, to remember that we are already freed from whatever happened before our birth, and can become free of whatever chains have been wrapped around us since. It is then possible to recall and confront our past life honestly and without fear, asking ourselves some important questions: What lies was I taught about people of color? What lies was I taught about white people? What inaccuracies have I learned about American history, especially the history of racism and slavery? How has my life been affected by this conditioning? How did I learn these lies? What influence do they still exert over me? Reach back and remember the lies and the liars, your feelings and how you came to feel that way. Our freedom from individual racism, our survival inside the prison is at stake. And so also is our ability to take part in the prison break that promises freedom from the prison itself.

Other Images of Individual Freedom

Our primary metaphor for racism and the overcoming of racism has been that of imprisonment and freedom. There are other helpful images. It will be useful in the context of this discussion to describe briefly three other images that are frequently used. Each of these is based on an understanding that racism is a force that produces brokenness in our humanity, and that the effort to overcome it is a way of restoring wholeness.

Insanity and Mental Health. Many psychologists believe that racism reflects problems of mental health, both individually and collectively in a society. Indeed, some years ago, under the Carter administration, the U.S. Department of Health, Education and Welfare classified racism as a manifestation of mental illness, and provided public funding for its treatment.

One of the reasons why racism is so difficult to analyze rationally is because it is a form of insanity. It is an expression of behavior by unstable individuals and societies. Seriously ill mental patients seek to confound those who are treating them with all sorts of behavioral tricks. One of these is a continual shifting and change of behavior so that it defies categorization. So also with expressions of racism. The moment a current behavior pattern is analyzed and categorized, it shifts, and its analysts are forced to begin their research all over again.

As the following excerpt from an article in the *New York Times* points out, psychiatrists and psychologists are developing new techniques for overcoming racism in individuals and the larger society:

> As racial violence continues . . . and more subtle prejudice permeates many American institutions, psychologists are refining their understandings of how bigotry develops and devising new ways to fight and prevent it.
>
> Some of the most promising techniques are aimed at grade-school children, whose biases have not had time to harden. But research has also led to a range of principles that can be used by any organization, whether university or corporation or city government or armed service, to change the atmosphere that leads to racial incidents.[9]

Addiction and Recovery. The United States is an addictive society. Not only alcohol and drugs, but many other societal problems such as overeating and consumerism are increasingly being seen as addictive behavior. There is a sense in which racism can also be understood as addictive behavior. A primary tenet in this understanding of racism is that addictive behavior is an illness rather than a conscious act of misbehavior. Treatment, therefore, is not through guilt and punishment, but through therapy and healing.

The following excerpt of an article by Ed Kinane provides a glimpse of how our understanding of racism can be aided through its treatment as addictive behavior:

> My Name is Ed. I'm a Racist.
>
> I recently went with a friend to a meeting of Alcoholics Anonymous. Before each person spoke she said, "My name is _____ . I'm an alcoholic." AA knows that recovery requires acknowledging one's illness; denial makes recovery impossible. What follows isn't about drinking, but about a more widespread disease. Before I say more, I want to introduce myself: "My name is Ed. I'm a racist."
>
> No, I'm not flaunting my bigotry, nor being cleverly rhetorical, nor tormenting myself with guilt. I'm acknowledging that I've been deeply conditioned by a society that is permeated with racism and that recovery is the task of a lifetime.

> AA teaches that alcohol is cunning; so too is racism. Just as it is hard to admit alcoholism, so too is it hard to admit racism—thanks to our stereotyped notion of what racism is . . .[10]

The treatment methods of Alcoholic Anonymous and similar groups provide us with useful tools for understanding and overcoming racism. As "recovering racists," we must move from denial to acknowledgment of the disease; from acknowledgment to admitting our helplessness; from admitting our helplessness to accepting responsibility with the help of God and others; from accepting responsibility to recovery—one day at a time. A recovering racist, like a recovering alcoholic, is never completely cured, but is always advancing in recovery, living a lifetime as a recovering racist.

Guilt and Forgiveness. Guilt and forgiveness have already been discussed in earlier pages. They are inevitably connected with the metaphors of imprisonment and freedom. However, it is important also to reflect on independent insights and perceptions about racism and the overcoming of racism in terms of guilt and forgiveness, especially as seen from a theological perspective.

From the perspective of the Christian faith, an act of repentance is more than feeling sorry for a sin and through absolution having no further responsibility for it. Repentance is, rather, both the decision to turn away from a sin and the process of carrying out that decision. It is a conversion, an act of turning around and moving in another direction. Turning around and moving away like this is not a one-time act but a continuing process. It is a retracing of our steps. Contrary to popular belief, to be forgiven does not mean that it is all right to forget. The forgiven person remembers the sin, and because of the forgiveness tries not to sin again and also tries to correct the behavior that caused the sin in the first place. Repentance and forgiveness not only restore a person to wholeness but give a person the ability to own up to present and past sins, to make restitution, and to participate in restoring wholeness to the world.

This understanding of guilt and forgiveness can be applied directly to racism. Guilt and repentance for racism extend far beyond feeling sorry for it and being freed from further responsibility through absolution. Rather, repentance is a turning away from racism. It is a conversion in which one turns around and moves in another direction, retracing one's steps. To be forgiven for one's racism does not mean that one may forget. The forgiven person remembers the sin of racism and because of forgiveness is enabled to try not to sin again and to correct his or her behavior. Repentance and forgiveness for racism not only restore a person to wholeness but give that person the ability to own up to the sins of racism of the past and present, to make restitution for racism, and to participate in restoring wholeness to the rest of the world.

Freedom Outside the Walls

As we have seen, it is possible for individuals to be free, though still confined to the prison of racism. No matter what the influences of past conditioning or the pressures of present institutional forces, no matter how much we are pressured to participate unwillingly in the actions of corporate racism, it is possible to be a free, forgiven, and whole person. Though free, we are still far from being fully satisfied. We are still in pain; we still know and feel our continued oppression and the oppression we are forced to bring upon others. In our freedom, continued imprisonment becomes more and more intolerable, and so we yearn and work for complete release.

The second dimension of freedom is the elimination of the prison itself: breaking out, destroying its dehumanizing power and its confining forces. But this requires corporate action. It is not possible to escape from the prison alone. There is no place to go. There are only different ways of working for elimination of the prison, as free persons operating from the inside. There are three ways in which elimination of the prison calls for corporate action, for joining together inside the prison. They will each be addressed here and in the remaining chapters of the book.

First, corporate action in destroying the prison of racism requires uniting with people of color, as well as learning to follow their leadership. This will be an important and consistent part of our discussion, reflection, and action, for it is a matter of great difficulty for us. As white people we have been conditioned throughout our history to assume that we are the natural leaders of people of color, and that their leadership cannot be as effective as ours. In the words of a Black South African, "There are two kinds of white people who want to help end apartheid in South Africa. One kind wants to lead Black people to freedom; the other knows that it is Black people who will lead South Africa to freedom. The first kind cannot follow Black leadership, the second can." The situation is identical to ours in the United States. The leaders in the struggle to combat racism are people of color. We who are white must learn to trust and follow them.

Second, corporate action requires that we address our white sisters and brothers with a new sense of mission. Our identity as white people and our sense of unity with other white people become critically important. A basic requirement for effective work against racism is a sense of kinship with white people and a deep desire for white people's liberation from racism's imprisonment. We can learn much about this from people of color. They have discovered the importance of recovering racial and ethnic identity and unity in order to gain freedom. Not only has it become necessary to emphasize the richness of their culture and the strength of their personal identity, but also to insist that freedom and progress depend on unity and interdependence. These same principles can be applied to us in our "mission to white people."

Once, in an interracial discussion, a white man tried to convince an African American that he was different from the rest of the white people and not racist like the rest. The African American responded that one of the differences he saw between white people and African Americans was in the way in which most African Americans identified with their own people. "White people," he went on to say, "more often than not think they have to disassociate themselves from other white people in order to establish their identity, whereas African Americans are more likely to find their identity only as they relate to their own people. Look at me," he said. "By your standards, if I were to judge myself only as an individual, I would see myself as a successful and free person. I have a Ph.D., $60,000-a-year salary, a house, a couple of cars, a good family, a promising future. The greatest temptation for a person such as myself is to be come a traitor to my people, and say that I am free. But I will only be free when my people are free. And until then, I am committed to using my life to work for our freedom."

What do we have to do as white people to be able to say the same thing about ourselves? Our dedication to the freedom of our white sisters and brothers must become an open and honest issue in our discussions and in our future agendas.

Third, corporate action means working against corporate and systemic forms of racism. Although our discussion of individual racism has been important, we must recognize that even our individual imprisonment is an act of corporate institutional racism. Even more, we must comprehend that the power of racism to control, exploit, and destroy people of color is entrenched in the policies, practices, structures, and foundations of our institutions. These are the formidable walls to which we now turn.

Summary

In this chapter we have seen how individual racists are created by the systemic empowerment and perpetuation of our personal prejudices. Isolation, anesthesia, privilege, and conditioning education are the forces that bind us to the prison of racism. There are two dimensions of freedom for individual racists. The first is freedom within the prison, a freedom to resist and work for racism's dismantling. The second is complete freedom through the prison's destruction. This can only happen with a nationwide and global assault on the structures of institutional racism.

4

INSTITUTIONAL RACISM

> *There are, after all, no significant formal*
> *institutions in American life—not the*
> *government, not the national economy, not*
> *the church, and not education—that are not*
> *controlled by Whites.*
> *—Benjamin Bowser and Raymond Hunt*

A society is composed of a great number of institutions. They may be either private or public, but all are interconnected through their common task of helping the society to function. Institutions and corporate systems give expression to the organized activities of a community and serve its various needs. In a representative democracy like the United States, public institutions are theoretically representative of the will of its citizens, and serve their needs in a fair and egalitarian manner.

The institutions in our society are countless, yet each purports to serve a specific and identifiable clientele. Governmental institutions claim as their clientele all citizens within their jurisdiction. The House of Representatives, the Senate, and all its committees and offices; the Supreme Court and the separate and intricate units of the judicial system; the Executive Branch of government, the White House, and the hundreds upon hundreds of departments and bureaucratic offices of government—each functions as a separate institutional entity. Each of the fifty states replicates the federal image with its offices and agencies; every city, town, and county does likewise; each city hall, library, police department, hospital, and museum is a public institution. Each and every business and industry in our nation, large and small, is an institution with factories, offices, or retail stores. Within the communications industry, the media and each newspaper, radio and TV station, magazine, and computer network is an institution. Every school, college, and university, every art gallery, dance studio, band, and orchestra, and a thousand, thousand more groups are institutions. The list seems almost as numerous as the stars and constellations. Each institution, at least theoretically, represents and collectively acts in the name of those whom it claims as its members, its owners, its clientele, or its citizens.

These are the institutions of which we speak when we address the question of institutional racism. The formidable restraints of racism's prison are not composed of individuals, but of these corporate structures. The walls that surround us, confining us within and oppressing others without, are improperly and unjustly functioning institutions and systems of the white society. These are the forces that make us, as individuals, into racists. They are the forces that transform individual prejudice into corporate racist action. Through these institutions, the subordination and exploitation of America's people of color take place.

In this chapter, we will concern ourselves specifically with the task of understanding our imprisonment in institutional racism as it exists in the United States. First, we will look at our nation's past history of direct, legalized institutional racism, and the recent successful struggle to render it illegal. Then we will explore how racism has continued in indirect ways that are not only illegal but also to a great extent self-perpetuating and out of control. Finally, we will examine the different levels of racism that exist in any given institution, and what is required to bring about change at each level.

The purpose of analyzing the racism in these corporate structures is not mere academic pursuit. Rather it is to continue the process of de-anesthetizing our consciousness and of dealing with our feelings of frustration and anger. It is to personalize the corporate actions of our society's institutions: to become keenly aware not only of their racist results, but also of our participation in bringing these results about. A legitimate result of our anger can be organized action aimed toward exposing, confronting, and eradicating institutional racism. Through this process, you and I can become better equipped to join with others in collective action for significant change in the racist behavior of institutions.

Institutional Power at Work

When we examine institutional racism, the issue of power must once again be emphasized. Remember that racism is the power to enforce one's prejudices. As our nation oppresses its people of color, our personal bigotry and prejudice do not cause the primary damage. Rather, the damage is done by racism that has been institutionally empowered and is administered in seemingly impersonal ways. The simple reality is that the institutions listed above, which theoretically represent in a fair and equal way all of their citizens, members, or clientele, do not do so.

We could understand this better if we could feel what it is like to be a person of color on the receiving end of educational, housing, welfare, police, labor, political, and economic institutional activity. Then we would know that racism is far more than the actions of an individual teacher, real estate agent, social worker, police officer, ward leader, or bank teller, as devastating as that can be. It is the structure, organization, policies, and practices of the institutions that these people represent. These institutions have power to control lives, but people of color have no reciprocal power to direct and control the institutions. Consciously and unconsciously, these institutions have been designed to benefit the majority of Americans, to the detriment and oppression of the minority.

But it is not simply that these institutions control and exploit people of color. They do it in our name! We also, not only people of color, are controlled and exploited by institutional racism. We participate in their actions, whether we want to or not.

They do it for us, whether we want them to or not. It is incorrect to assume that our institutions act without personal accountability, and that we, therefore, have no responsibility for their actions. It is not true that if we disagree we can simply disassociate ourselves by disclaiming responsibility. When we believe this, we are not only deceiving ourselves but are also voluntarily decreasing our power to bring about change.

It is theoretically impossible for a democratic society to function on any level without the acceptance and agreement of the majority. When a new law is enacted by a representative body such as a city council or the United States Congress; when a section of the city is re-zoned for industrial or residential use; when automobile manufacturers annually change their models and increase their prices; when decisions are made to raise or lower social security or welfare benefits, or to raise or lower military spending; or when any of a thousand such decisions are made that affect our daily lives, our silent and passive acceptance is interpreted as agreement.

When the real estate and housing industries continue to build, sell, and rent in patterns of residential segregation; when business, industry, and labor persist in discriminatory hiring and promotions, either by outright rejection of people of color or by playing games with standards and qualifications; when schools continue to be racially unbalanced, with quality education withheld from minority students; when the media project images of African Americans, Hispanics, Native Americans, and Asians that fulfill our expectations and reinforce our prejudices, our silence or the mildness of our protests suggests to these institutions and agencies that we condone their actions.

And they are often right in making such assumptions. For the result of all the conditioning and brainwashing described in the previous chapter is that from within our anesthetized and comfortable prison, the vast majority of us do benefit from and condone their actions. Our institutions are designed to benefit those of us who are white and middle class. In this way, we are shielded from their effects on others. As we have stated, their services to us provide the curtains that cover the bars in our prisons; it is a reward to us for accepting things as they are and not demanding that conditions for others be changed. As long as we accept these favors, we will be happy inside our prison and will not rebel against our enslavement or object to being used for the corporate control and exploitation of others.

Moreover, most of us participate directly in one or more of these institutions and actually help them carry out their actions. As teachers, doctors, lawyers, police, clergy, business executives, real estate agents, and bankers, or even as assistants, secretaries, file clerks, and line workers, or in whatever other way we are involved in institutional life, we share in the administration of institutional racism. As we turn to a more detailed examination, let us maintain our awareness of the power these organizations wield over people of color, who are the target of institutional racism, and over ourselves, who are simultaneously its prisoners, its functionaries, and its beneficiaries.

Hate Groups: A Terrifying Distraction

The most visible and well-known organizations that practice institutional racism in the United States are the hate groups that publicly espouse white supremacy and violence against people of color. They include the Ku Klux Klan, Aryan Nations, Skinheads, and other neo-Nazi supremacist movements. Although they are described as fringe groups, it is important to recognize that in many ways they act out the beliefs and values of a much larger number of people who quietly agree with and encourage their activities. As Michael Omi and Howard Winant report, many of these groups become even more frightening by taking on a higher degree of political involvement:

> In the past the target of such actions were minority groups themselves—groups which had to be terrorized into "knowing their place." In the 1980's, however, the target has shifted to the federal government. . . . Targeting the federal government is a direct response to the racial activism of the state in the 1960's. Busing, affirmative action, and other egalitarian measures have created, in the white supremicist view, a racially unjust society. The society has become "polluted" and the federal government, and liberalism in particular, are responsible. Pastor Richard G. Butler of the Aryan

Nations preaches such a view at his Church of Jesus Christ Christian in Idaho:

"When the Declaration of Independence talks about 'one people,' it is not talking about a nation made for Asia, Africa, India [or] the Soviet Union. That's a document based on a Christian people. We have watched like frightened sheep as do-gooders sniveling about the underprivileged gleefully grabbed our children by the nape of the neck and rubbed their faces in the filth to create equality."[1]

One dare not underestimate the significance and danger of these fringe hate groups. Especially in recent years a renewed increase in their popularity has been paralleled by a dramatic increase in racial violence and hate crimes throughout the whole society. The Southern Poverty Law Center's Klanwatch Project, in Montgomery, Alabama, has recorded the course of white supremacist movements over the previous decade. They identify 230 organized hate groups operating throughout the nation.[2] This is but the tip of an iceberg; these supremacist movements are indicators of far more serious problems that lie beneath the surface.

Although these groups are an extremely serious problem in themselves, concern about their activities can also be used to distract from less obvious, but far more destructive forms of institutional racism. Far more dangerous are the legitimate and polite public institutions at the center of society that, by self-righteously contrasting themselves with these fringe hate groups, effectively draw attention away from their own racist practices.

Economics at the Center

Below the tip of the iceberg, the massive bulk of institutional racism is composed neither of hate groups nor of the hate crimes that are regularly and dramatically reported in the daily news. Institutional racism is, rather, a colossal structure that affects each facet of our daily lives. And at the core of institutional racism is economics.

More than ever, the arena for struggle against institutional racism has shifted to the marketplace. The issue is no longer who may eat in a restaurant, but who can afford to; not who is allowed to live in a neighborhood, but who can afford the mortgage or rent. The issue of employment, particularly on the low-income end of the labor market, is not only training and skill development, but whether there is a job. And, in the political arena, particularly in our large cities, the issue is less whether a person of color can be elected to political office but whether there will be an economic base to work with after the election.

We have said that institutional racism is fundamentally an economic issue. There seems to be a never-ending debate between Marxists and non-Marxists as to whether racism is simply another form of classism. The intensity and complexity of the debate often cover up the simple fact that, no matter where one stands, the primary result of racism is unequal financial advantage and power. One does not have to be a Marxist to recognize the interrelationship of racism and classism. Nor does one have to concede that alongside economics stand other important expressions of institutional racism. It should be clear, however, that economic issues are central in the struggle for racial justice.

Unmasking the Institutions

Institutional racism is practiced in two ways, which we will call "direct" and "indirect." Direct institutional racism, as the name suggests, is always conscious and intentional; it is openly and publicly practiced without apology or shame. It has also been, until recently, quite legal. Indirect institutional racism may be intentional or unintentional. When it is intentional, indirect racism is deliberately disguised or hidden so that the public will be unaware of it. When unintentional, indirect racism is far more complex. It can exist as though it has a life of its own and is extremely difficult to eradicate.

Direct Institutional Racism

Conscious, intentional racism, practiced openly, backed by the force of the law and without danger of serious disapproval, was once the only form of institutional racism. Since it was for the most part acceptable and legal until the 1960s, there was little need for any other kind. At first, the institution of slavery required very little legal definition or control. But soon a need developed for a body of laws to control the behavior of the slaves and even, to a certain extent, of the slavemasters. After emancipation, and especially after the end of reconstruction, numerous laws were created for effective segregation and control. Likewise, a body of laws and a number of institutions were created to control Native Americans, whether on or off the reservations. African Americans and Native Americans were the chief targets, but Hispanics and Asians were also largely excluded from eating, sleeping, residing, walking, riding, working, playing, worshiping, voting, or doing virtually anything at the same time or place in which white people were doing these same things.

It has only been thirty years or so since this has changed. On the one hand, it is a matter of burning anger and shame that a system of legal apartheid was held intact in the United States until so recently. On the other hand, there is cause for great joy that this legal system has been so thoroughly discredited and that so much of it has been dismantled. However, this sense of joy is once again covered with even greater anger and shame in the face of the reality that although this legal base for the most part no longer exists, institutional racism continues to flourish.

It is impossible to comprehend how institutional racism functions today without understanding its connection with the legalized system that only so recently was dissolved. Every practice of institutional racism still in force today is directly linked to those conscious, intentional, and legal activities of the past. Furthermore, each conscious decision can be historically traced, and its continuing effect on the present-day life of institutions can be identified. This concept that every act of institutional racism has deliberate and traceable origins is important for at least three reasons:

1. We are a people whose memories have been shortened by amnesia and anesthesia and whose knowledge of history has been distorted. An entirely new generation of people has reached adulthood since 1960. Many have little awareness of the civil rights movement or of

the legal system of institutional racism that existed before that time. They have never known separate toilets and water fountains, segregated buses, restaurants, and accommodations, and all the other insulting and exploitative indignities. This recent history dare not be forgotten, particularly since it still exerts such a powerful influence over us.

2. Institutional racism as practiced today with subtlety and sophistication often seems both innocent and innocuous unless it is recognized as the successor in disguise to the deliberate and direct institutional racism of the past. Rather than being eliminated, racism has been driven underground. Because it is illegal and no longer as acceptable as it formerly was, it must be practiced in more subtle and hidden forms. The results, however, are no less harmful. Today's racism cannot be understood or confronted without comprehending its deliberate and intentional origins.

3. Many institutional leaders are sincere in their desire for racial harmony, but they deny the existence of racist practices in their institutions. They do not understand what causes racial problems, and are honestly not conscious or intentional in their racism. Such persons must become aware of their institution's racism, and of their own personal imprisonment in its corporate forms. To achieve such awareness, they must, first of all, understand the history of their own institution's public and conscious racist practices—a history that still profoundly influences their institution's life.

Tracing Deliberate Decisions: An Example

Residential segregation by housing and the real estate industry is an excellent example of deliberate and historically traceable institutional racism. In nearly every American city and town we will find a separate area, a "ghetto," where African Americans, Hispanics, Asians, or Native Americans were permitted to purchase or rent housing. These segregated communities are not there by accident. Moreover, our own communities have not remained virtually all white because "those people" did not want to live there.

These communities are what they are because of institutional decisions that were consciously made and are on public record. These decisions were made by the political bodies holding power in each city, town, or country—probably the city council, the board of supervisors, or a powerful semipublic or private group such as the real estate board. The decisions are usually part of the public record and, more often than not, are easily traceable. If you can find out the approximate year that African Americans or other persons of color came to live in your town, for example, you will probably find somewhere in the public records for that year (at the city hall, the public library, or in the records of the real estate board) a hasty decision as to where these new arrivals would be permitted to live. In the records of the real estate board, you might even discover the penalty for violating these decisions.

Particularly in the years after World War II, many decisions were made relating to housing and residential segregation. It was then that suburbs were born, when major residential developments grew up on the fringes of most cities, and a vast exodus from city to suburb redefined residential America. The movement to the suburbs also solved another problem that faced government officials at the time: what to do with the great numbers of African Americans and other people of color who had migrated to the northern and western cities during the war to fill jobs made available by the war effort. During the war, they had generally been placed in temporary housing, but now there was need for more permanent quarters. The inner core of the nation's northern cities had been built in the late nineteenth and early twentieth centuries to house waves of European immigrants who were filling the jobs created by America's industrial expansion. That housing—fifty or more years old, and already showing much wear and tear—was to be turned into the overcrowded inner city racial ghettos we know today.

In the records of city councils, real estate boards, and banks in virtually every northern and western city can be found the decisions that were made to create a racial ghetto within the inner city, section by section, block by block. Records of housing inspectors generally demonstrate that most of the areas that were abandoned by whites and left to people of color were already at the edge of deterioration and decay. Yet it was an easy task in the years that followed to convince white people that the "invasion" of Blacks and other minorities caused the neighborhood to fall to pieces. In reality, you will discover, it was the result of conscious actions by white institutions. Title companies and the banking industry usually participated in or cooperated with such ghetto-creating decisions, especially in areas where housing purchases, rather than just rentals, were possible. Internal banking decisions were made to refrain from lending money to persons of color for mortgages or repairs unless the housing was in the designated area. "Blockbusting" was another tactic carried out by the real estate industry during this time. Playing on the insecurity of white homeowners, real estate agents bought up entire blocks of city housing by spreading rumors about Black buyers who were "invading" the neighborhood.

Another practice of suburban tract developers, especially during the post-war years, was the placing of restrictive covenants in deeds, forbidding any home in a given tract or development to be sold to anyone but whites. These deeds often included a provision to which more than 90 percent of the original owners had to consent before the restrictive covenant could be changed. The following restrictive clause from a deed of a suburban tract development in California illustrates this practice.

CLAUSE XI: Limitation of Use and Occupancy: No part of said property or any building erected, constructed, or maintained thereon shall be occupied or resided upon by any person not wholly of white or Caucasian race. Domestic servants who are members of other than the white or Caucasian race may live in or occupy the premises where their employer resides.

Such covenants were standard practice throughout the country, and they did not get into the deeds by accident. They were conscious decisions by the tract developers, and for a long time they were upheld by the courts. For example, the decision of the U.S. Supreme Court (Shelly vs. Kramer, 334U.S. 1, 1948) which revised the ruling of the Supreme Court of the state of Michigan. The latter originally held restrictive covenants unenforceable by state courts. The higher court held that such agreements were enforceable.

Finally, in 1953, the U.S. Supreme Court (Barrow vs. Jackson, 346U.S. 249, 1953) ruled that it is a violation of equal protection and due process clauses of the 14th Amendment for a state court to award damages for the violation of a restrictive covenant. By that time, however, the nature of America's suburbs had already been determined, and despite great efforts by many fair housing groups, it has been impossible to change in any significant way the exclusiveness of white residential communities.

A southern version of these traceable corporate decisions to create a Black ghetto exists in Miami Florida. Running through the entire area called Coconut Grove on the South End of Miami are the remains of an eight-foot stone wall, built to separate Black and white residential neighborhoods. Resolution 745, adopted at the Miami City Planning Board meeting of July 21, 1941, reads as follows: "A resolution recommending that the establishment of a permanent dividing line between white and colored occupancy in the area north of Grand Avenue and east of Douglas Road." There are also later resolutions that describe the placement, size, access, roads, and responsibility for maintenance of the wall. The wall's remains still stand, but few citizens of Coconut Grove remember its original purpose, or the decisions that created it.

Discrimination in housing is no longer legal. But the mold was cast; the prison door was already locked, and no one has yet found the key to open it. We still remain in residentially segregated communities, and few changes are taking place. Not only are we controlled by the decisions and lies of the past, but—as we shall shortly see—these same institutions continue to practice racism in more subtle and hidden ways. The point is that today's residential segregation is not an accident. Our separate ghettos were intentionally constructed, street by street, block by block, community by community. We cannot comprehend our present situation, or plan strategies for the future unless we have a clear understanding of our imprisonment by the past.

Unmasking Other Disguises

Residential segregation is just one example of deliberate and historically traceable institutional racism, and how it has affected race relations in the United States. Almost any area of public and private institutional life will yield similar examples of consciously decided, historically traceable racism. The segregation and poor quality of ghetto schools were produced by intentional design. You can trace those decisions in the public records of your board of education. The tiny number of people of color holding management positions in business and industry is also no accident. Check out your own company's history for the corporate decisions that helped to create this situation. White exclusiveness in most labor unions, high crime rates among people of color, conflict between police and communities of color, predominance of people of color in prison populations—these and a thousand other manifestations of institutional racism can be understood only by recognizing that our current problems are directly traceable to institutional decisions of an earlier day.

The painful realities of the present are rooted firmly in the past. The consciously racist decisions of the institutions related to your work or your residential life can and should be traced to their source. Events, times, people, and decisions can be discovered and should be described in detail. With such knowledge it is possible to establish the continuity between public decisions of the past and today's hidden practices of indirect racism.

Indirect Racism Takes Over

With the passing of the civil rights legislation of the 1960s, the major part of legalized institutional racism was eliminated. At least according to the law, people of color could now eat, sleep, work, play, worship, vote, own property, and do anything at the same time and the same place as white people. From a legal point of view, the long struggle had paid off. Direct institutional racism had been effectively eliminated within the United States. How-

ever, even before the victory could be properly celebrated, it became clear that institutional racism was not coming to an end but
was going underground. Today it is clear that the end of *de jure*
(legalized) racism has failed to bring about the end of *de facto* (actual) racism. On the contrary, as stated in chapter one, a fair and
equitable society is as elusive as ever. Direct institutional racism
has been replaced by indirect forms that are, in many ways, more
powerful and destructive than before, if for no other reason than
because they are more difficult to detect and eliminate.

Indirect racism can be voluntary or involuntary. It may be
the deliberate continuation of former direct practices, implemented through hidden and deceptive ways. Or it may be that an
institution's history of deliberate racism is so rooted in its structures and so imprisoned by decisions made decades, even centuries ago that they perpetuate themselves despite serious efforts to
bring about change. As we shall see, such "involuntary" racism
is the most difficult to eradicate. But first, let us look at deliberate
indirect racism.

Many devious methods have been developed to deliberately perpetuate racism in indirect ways. Individually and collectively, the managers of America's public and private institutions
have created sophisticated methods of hiding illegal racist practices. Although many people are dedicated to bring about
changes that will help achieve a racially just society, it is impossible to exaggerate the extent of the duplicity and treachery still
being practiced by many of our nation's private and public leaders in order to control and exploit people of color in our society.
The blame for these practices, however, must be shared by all of
us for actively or passively condoning them and willingly accepting their benefits.

Instances of deliberate indirect racism are to be found in
nearly every area in which direct racism at one time flourished.
Let us look again at residential segregation. When it was still legal, the real estate industry simply refused to show or sell property to a person of color. Now, however, there are ingenious
schemes and systems of "steering" customers toward or away
from locations that have been primarily designated for one particular racial group. Likewise, banks that once gave or refused

mortages to anyone they chose, or designated by fiat the composition of entire communities, have created such strategies as "redlining" to achieve the same results. Extensive studies of U.S. major cities from 1980 to 1990 have documented dramatic racial disparities in mortgage lending:

> They found that neighborhoods with at least 80% Black residents received 60% fewer mortgage loans per 1,000 separately owned housing properties (houses, apartment buildings, condos) than neighborhoods with fewer than 5% Black residents. When each neighborhood's income, wealth, average house value, vacancy rate, number of bank branches, new housing development, and ten other variables were taken into account, they were left with no explanation other than race itself for the remaining 24% shortfall in mortgage lending in predominantly minority neighborhoods.

> Are loans in minority neighborhoods riskier? Atlanta's Citizens Trust Bank, a Black owned bank which made nearly all of its housing loans in minority neighborhoods, had the lowest default rate on real estate loans of any bank of its size in the nation in 1986.[3]

Employers who, not so long ago, could accept and reject persons of color according to their personal racist views, have learned to use other criteria to disqualify and exclude unwanted persons. Educational standards are manipulated, residential requirements are added, together with age, height, and weight limitations. Governmental elections and representative appointments have been influenced, if not controlled, by the secret gerrymandering of political boundaries. Of course, unlike decisions of the past, these equally deliberate decisions are rarely recorded and, therefore, seldom traceable. They are made quietly and secretly at lunch, on the golf course, and in the men's washroom.

The dismantling of deliberate indirect racism is not just a matter of detection and prosecution by those who enforce the law. Like moles that respond to threats by burrowing deeper into the ground, people who engage in such practices develop increasingly subtle and sophisticated methods of deception. Moreover, those who are responsible for enforcing the law generally have little enthusiasm for the rooting out of indirect racism. They are like spinning saucers that lose their momentum and must be set spinning again and again. Usually, it takes a dramatic racial tragedy—first a news media expose, then public indignation and anger, and finally the institution's embarrassment—to create new energy for one more effort to correct another instance of indirect institutional racism.

An additional problem is that not all of these practices are actually illegal. Often they are by-products of what is perceived as "good business." In the past two decades, for example, most major banks as well as many supermarket chains and other commercial businesses have closed their branches in poor urban communities. Should such decisions be judged simply on the basis of these corporations' financial bottom line? Or do they, in their role as service industries, also have responsibilities to the society, responsibilities that require more of them than the selection of a clientele that provides them with the highest profit? If, indeed, racism is measured by results, the message is clear. Such corporate decisions deny to people of color convenient access to products and services at the same prices that are available to the rest of society.

Here we enter into the area where indirect racism may be unintentional and caused involuntarily. Many manifestations of indirect racism occur as by-products of corporate policies. It may even be that while on one level an institution honestly seeks to be nondiscriminatory, on another level it continues intentional or unintentional indirect racism. As long as the practices alone are scrutinized, and not their results, they may appear to be, or even actually be, completely innocent of intentional racism. The results, however, are what count. If there are no significant changes in the discrimination, exclusion, or exploitation of people of color from the time when deliberate and direct racism was practiced, then racism is still at work.

Such indirect racism is evident when corporate executives, government officials, union leaders, and other institutional representatives justify their lack of success in hiring or upgrading employees of color. "We want to," they say, "but it is not our fault if we can't find qualified people." Whereas, in the past, people of color were denied training because of their race, today they are rejected because they lack the necessary qualifications. It is like hitting people over the head and then rejecting them because they have lumps on their heads. A process of deliberate and direct racism throughout our history created the conditions that prevented people of color from becoming properly educated and well qualified for a host of occupations. Now indirect racism rejects them because they are poorly educated and ill-trained. As long as we permit this situation to continue, we are responsible for the results.

The insurance industry provides another illustration of racism as an indirect by-product of corporate practices. Most insurance companies charge different rates depending on where one lives, and usually the dividing line between higher and lower rates follows the boundaries between white communities and communities of color. A by-product of such higher rates, though perhaps unintentional, is indirect racism. Insurance companies do not make an overt practice of charging people of color higher rates. However, insurance rates are higher where the risk is higher. And the risk of fire, auto theft, accident, and a hundred other insurance losses is higher in communities of color. Coincidence or racism? Both. Racism is measured by results, and the results are that people of color pay more. The racism that is a consequence of the seemingly neutral practice of charging rates according to risk is perceived only by those who understand the underlying reasons that poor urban communities are high-risk areas in the first place.

Summary

We have looked first of all at direct institutional racism, practiced primarily when racism was still legally protected. At that time deliberate and historically traceable decisions were made that imposed the current structure on our segregated and unequal society. We have learned that these structures are still being perpetuated in indirect ways that are to a great extent intentional, but sometimes unintentional.

In this section we have only begun to examine the unintentional indirect racism that seems to have a life of its own, thwarting all serious efforts to eliminate it. But before we examine this more closely, we must take one more step in our exploration: how to look at the various levels and expressions of racism within a specific institution or organization. To do this, we will examine the cross-section of a typical institution.

Levels of Institutional Racism

In every institution are three distinct levels at which racism may be operating: attitudes and actions of personnel; policies and practices; structures and foundations. The last is the deepest of the three, for it embodies an institution's purpose and the philosophical basis for its operation.

Frequently the only racism acknowledged by an institution is on the first level—that of personnel attitudes and behavior. In reality, the racism that exists on the other two levels is far more serious and difficult to deal with. As we examine these three levels, it will become clear that the degree of racism in an institution can vary from level to level. At the same time, the more deeply it exists, especially in the foundations of the institution, the more difficult it is to eradicate.

Racism in Personnel

Let us take the example of a police sergeant who is an outright bigot, a conscious and intentional racist. He never tries to understand people of color. He never deals with his fear and hostility. In his attitudes and behavior as a police officer, he is arrogant and rude toward people of color, and never fails to evoke negative responses from them. People of color learn from such officers that the police are racist. They do not, as a rule, make distinctions between the blue uniform and the person inside it. Nor do they generally make distinctions between one particular officer and others in the police department. One individual's racism is all it takes to make the entire police force appear to be racist.

Similarly, a teacher who is racist can make the entire school system appear to be racist. A bigoted court clerk or judge infects the entire legal system. A salesperson who shows hostility toward people of color will create the impression that everyone in the store is hostile and racist. In short, when a "person" is also "personnel," he or she personifies the institution. That is why one person who has not dealt with her or his individual racism can make an entire institution appear to be racist.

Nevertheless, of the three levels of institutional racism, that in personnel is the least difficult to identify and alleviate. It is possible, for example, to test and evaluate the attitudes and perceptions of an individual before hiring. Education and training programs can help existing personnel change attitudes and behavior. More people of color can be hired. Education and training programs can be developed to help multiracial staff relate well to one another. Finally, it is possible to fire someone who refuses to understand or change behavior.

Racism in Policy and Practice

However, changing the racial attitudes of personnel is not nearly enough. It is barely a beginning. Far more significant is the racism embedded in the policies and practices of the institution. Even to begin changing attitudes and behavior of personnel, for example, requires changes in the institution's personnel policies. Identifying and eliminating racism that is built into policies and practices is far more difficult, especially since so much of it exists as indirect racism, frequently unintentional, rather than the more easily discernible direct and intentional forms of racism.

Any institution is guided by a vast number of policies, some of which are informal and unofficial, and others that are formally acknowledged and theoretically practiced by everyone in the institution. An example of the former, which can affect racial justice within the institution, is that of personnel hiring requirements such as age, education, height, physical condition, and residence. Another example might be policies related to product quality, sales quotas, or the geographical boundaries served by the institution. An example of policies that are informal, perhaps unwritten and known only to a few, would be a separate advancement track for favored personnel or a private product listing for favored clients.

The personnel within an institution may be carrying out racist policies and practices without realizing it. Let us look at an insurance firm in New York City. The men and women employed by this firm have already been tested and received training to deal with their individual racism. They try to be sensitive and to eliminate manifestations of racism in their attitudes and behavior. Many are, in fact, persons of color. On the level of personnel, this insurance firm has achieved a record of excellence. However, this same institution has policies and practices that are racist, even though they are indirect and unintentional. These policies result in rates that are significantly higher in areas largely composed of people of color. When the institution's personnel implement these policies, they carry out the institution's corporate racism. Dick Gregory, the social activist comedian, describes a theoretical institution that has replaced all its white personnel with persons of color. However, its racist policies and practices have not been changed. Therefore, it will still be a white racist institution, completely administered by people of color acting the parts of white racists. This same phenomenon is described in a common African American saying: "A Black person in a blue uniform is still a white cop."

In identifying racism within an institution, it is also important to understand the distinction between policy and practice. An institution's practices may not correspond to its policies. Racism in practice may be the direct result of fulfilling racist policy. Or it may exist in contradiction to official policy or even in its absence. For example, a city police department may have a stated policy of equal protection for all neighborhoods, but its practice may be very different. A school district may have a policy that educational materials of equal quality be provided for every school, but in practice may be far from fulfilling this policy. A corporation may state that it locates housing for personnel on an equal basis, but in practice it may place white personnel in the white suburbs and personnel of color in the inner city.

Racism in institutional policies and practices can be eliminated. In developing a pluralistic institution it is crucial to eliminate every racist component of policy and practice and to redesign those policies and practices in a racially just and sensitive manner. Such recasting is both possible and essential. Racist results can be clearly identified and measured; policies can be changed; practices can be altered—all without coming into serious conflict with the underlying structures and foundations of an institution. However, as we now move to explore this final level of institutional racism, we should be aware that we are confronting racism in its deepest institutional expression.

Racism in Structures and Foundations

The third level of institutional racism is found in its structures and its very foundations. This is the most important of the three levels. Racism within this level is also the most difficult to eradicate. When an institution's racism is to be found predominantly within the first two levels, changes can be made without overwhelming difficulty. However, when dealing with the third level, in the structures and foundations of an institution, change is far more difficult to achieve. When a building develops serious problems in its structure, major renovations must be done. If the problems are in its foundations, it may be necessary to tear the building down and rebuild it from the bottom up. Likewise, in dealing with racism in an institution, when a serious problem exists in its structure, the process of change can be very complex. However, if racism is embedded in its very foundations, a rebuilding from the bottom up may be necessary.

By institutional "structures," we mean organizational units and divisions, administration and leadership design, methods of production, product or service delivery systems, area or service boundaries, the financial base, and similar elements. Structural racism can be built into the design or operation of any of these areas. It exists when the defined boundaries of an institution's services exclude people of color or do not serve them equally. It exists when the product or service is of inferior quality when provided to people of color. Higher insurance rates in the inner city, discussed earlier in this chapter, do not exemplify racism on the levels of personnel, policy or practice. Rather they are manifestations of structural racism.

Another instance of structural racism is when the leadership of a multiracial community or institution is either appointed by or solely accountable to a small, powerful minority (usually white) within the community or institution. The Chicago public school system, for example, is trying to eliminate such racism by restructuring local school boards so that they are elected by and responsible to the local community.

One final example: If the staff or leadership of a multiracial community or institution is predominately white and does not represent proportionately its membership, it is more than a problem of personnel or policy, it is a structural issue. One of the most common indicators of structural racism in institutions is when teachers in a school system, clergy or lay professionals in a church structure, or doctors, lawyers, elected officials, and others in a variety of community and institutional settings are not proportionately represented in the organizations they serve.

When we speak of an institution's "foundations," we mean its stated purposes, its historical traditions, the spiritual and moral teachings on which it is built, and its financial undergirding. If any of these are affected by racism, we must assume that the structures, practices, policies, and personnel of the institution will be similarly affected. An institution's foundational principles are usually recorded in its constitution, articles of incorporation, charter, historical records, or sacred documents. Often these documents will provide some clues to an institution's underlying perspective.

Obvious examples of such institutions are the Ku Klux Klan and other similar white supremacist organizations and political parties. Such groups are clearly inundated with racism in their deepest foundations: purpose, historical tradition, spiritual teaching, and financial base. Usually, however, the situation is far more complex and controversial. The foundational base of every organization that has developed in the United States, including the government itself, has been infected and corrupted by racism. The question centers on the degree to which it has been affected and whether the institution is able to rebuild and strengthen its foundational base.

Some examples: Our justice system is staggering under the load of criminal prosecutions. This, despite the obvious racism that exists in virtually all aspects of the task. How much of this burden reflects the foundational base of the criminal justice system? To what degree has it become the very purpose of the police and the courts to protect that part of America that is mostly white from the other part of America that is mostly people of color?

Another example, even more difficult and controversial: If the private institutions that provide products and services to American consumers (banks, supermarkets, hospitals, and the like) do so on the basis of profit, resulting in the racially unjust distribution of products and services, where does one lay the blame? Are we describing racism in the foundational base of our economic system?

A final example: The Christian church has as its stated purpose, directed by its sacred documents, the task of promoting racial justice. Yet it is the most segregated institution in the United States. Does this reflect racism only on levels of personnel, policy, or structure? Or does it suggest that racism has become a part of the very foundational base of the church?

The Prison Once Again

On the level of racism in structures and foundations of our institutions, we are able to examine more closely the indirect racism that seems to continue despite all serious efforts to dislodge it. It is here that we finally come to grips with the reality that has haunted us since the beginning: that things are not changing. Racism is not lessening in America. Racial segregation is more severe than ever before, especially in our cities. Poverty rates for people of color are rigid and unchanging. The public schools and public health systems, the criminal justice and prison systems all remain at the brink of complete bankruptcy.

Why? What is it about these structures and systems that has resisted all efforts at change? For the efforts have indeed been significant. During the past decades since the civil rights movement, serious attempts have been made within public and private institutions to correct their racism. Government and private industry have sought to deal with unemployment and underemployment. In the schools, many attempts have been made to change the quality of education in communities of color. There have been housing programs, drug and crime programs, programs of family development and birth control—the list goes on and on. But even with the best intentions and the most innovative programs, we have learned only that institutional racism is not easily changed. It is like pushing down the bubble of a balloon and having two more bubbles pop up elsewhere.

Can it be true that racism is totally out of control—out of control even of the racists? Is there a point in the life of an institution or even a whole society when certain deliberate patterns of behavior become permanently embedded, taking on a life of their own? Can it be that in its final form, indirect racism becomes so entrenched that the halting of identifiable racist activities has no effect, that it continues on its own energy and under its own directives, and that taking corrective action only causes it to alter its course? At that stage, racism in one institution might develop connections with other institutions, like the limbs of a single body, which are connected by veins, nerves, and muscles and virtually impossible to separate from one another. This would help to explain the great difference of opinion about the best starting point for correcting the effects of institutional racism. And it would explain why efforts to eradicate racism in one institution seem to strengthen it in another.

Directions for a Prison Break

But, it is not racism that is out of control. Throughout this book we have been using the imagery of a prison. We have suggested that the system of racism is a prison for us as well as for people of color. We have insisted that we have been trying to solve the wrong problem and to change the wrong people. It is we who need to be changed. It is we, not racism, who are out of control. This is very difficult for us to accept because we who are white, and particularly those of us who are male, have such an overwhelming need to be in control of every situation.

The most important question is not who is in control of racism, but who is in control of bringing about change. Whether or not we have lost control of our racism, we cannot be in control of dismantling it. We are the ones who need to be changed. This is as much a statement of theological truth as it is a practical statement on how to change racism in an institution. As a theological truth, it affirms that we need to be set free, to be healed, to be made whole again. It is a confession of belief in a God who is involved in restoring the creation and reconciling that which has been irreconcilable. As a practical statement, it insists that we need the leadership, guidance, and collective participation of racism's victims to develop the means of dismantling racism in its institutional expressions.

The first practical step toward overcoming institutional racism is the recognition that people of color hold the key to change. Leadership and direction can only come from them. People of color understand racism far better than we do, and they know what needs to be done to eliminate it. Thus, the first step toward breaking the chains of this prison is to recognize that we cannot be in charge of the changing. The combating and elimination of racism from our nation's institutions is a joint venture with people of color, and they, not we, know how this can best be accomplished. The following words of Jim Wallis help in understanding this issue:

> The strategies for how black people must confront and finally overcome the ever-changing face of white racism in America must always originate within the black community itself. White allies have and can continue to play a significant role in the struggle against racism when black autonomy and leadership are sufficiently present to make possible a genuine partnership. But an even more important task for white Americans is to examine ourselves, our institutions, and our society for the ugly plague of racism. . . .
>
> White racism in white institutions must be eradicated by white people and not just black people. In fact, white racism is primarily a white reponsibility.[4]

Thus, an effective approach to change within an institution begins with this principle: that people of color on the staff and among the membership, whether few or many in number, know more than anyone else what needs to be changed, whether it be in the areas of personnel, policies, practices, structures, or foundations. And they know what the institution would be like if it were no longer racist. This is the key. This is the formula for a prison break. If we want a society without racism, then the power to undo that racism must belong to those from whom power has been taken. Of course, it is not easy for us to relinquish that power. And, even if we do, the task of undoing racism, step by step, will be a frustrating and painful task. The prison walls of institutional racism are very high and very thick. We must recognize that there is no quick fix, even if we address the task openly and honestly in a joint venture with people of color.

The good news is that we need not be locked forever into this prison. Racism is not out of control. The walls can be broken down, block by block, step by step. That which has been built can be dismantled. In the final chapter we will discuss further steps and resources. But now, let us turn to cultural racism.

5

CULTURAL RACISM

America is an unfinished nation—the
product of a badly bungled process of
inter-group cultural fusion.
—Harold Cruse
The Crisis of the Negro Intellectual

The third form of racism that we will explore is cultural racism. In recent years, this issue has become increasingly important as culture has become a major factor in the developing of new alternatives for racial justice in church and society. A racially just society must be built on a multicultural foundation.

"Culture" suggests to most people a narrowly defined area including music, art, and dance, usually of the so-called classical variety. However, we are concerned here with much more. Culture includes nearly every aspect of a people's lifestyle, certainly its music, art, and dance, but also whatever else is distinctive about that society's values, language, literature, religion, food, clothing, and other behaviors.

In addition to the expected narrow definition of culture, "acquaintance with and taste in fine arts and humanities," Webster has a second definition, "the integrated pattern of human behavior that includes thought, speech, action, and artifacts and depends upon man's [sic] capacity for learning and transmitting knowledge to succeeding generations," and a third, particularly relevant to this discussion: "the customary beliefs, social forms, and material traits of a racial, religious, or social group."[1]

As we begin the discussion, it is also necessary to make a clear distinction between the terms *race* and *culture*. Persons of the same race can be from different cultural backgrounds. Culture is an outgrowth not only of race but also of religious, social, or ethnic identity. For example, within Africa there are a number of vastly different cultures and subcultures. This is likewise true in Asia, Latin America, and Europe. The terms *multicultural* and *crosscultural* reflect, therefore, the intersecting of other group characteristics besides race.

On the other hand, racial segregation in the United States has created five distinctly separated racial/cultural groupings. The five groups are the Native Americans who are indigenous to North America; Hispanics from South America, Central America, and the Caribbean; Asians who come from a variety of Asian countries; African Americans, whose roots are in many African countries—some by way of the Caribbean; and European Americans. Many add a sixth culture, the Pacific Islanders. Even though each of these racial/cultural groupings is composed of many originally separate historic cultural, ethnic, and tribal subgroupings, racial segregation is responsible for the development of these five uniquely American racial/cultural expressions.

The five groupings have also been greatly affected in another way by racism and other forms of exploitation. It is possible to speak of subcultures of oppression, poverty, or survival. These subcultures become the context for the preservation and development of culture. Some of the most powerful expressions of culture are created in the fires of suffering and exploitation. Two examples that come immediately to mind are the Negro spiritual and soul food.

In this chapter, we will examine cultural racism, and in particular, the separate development of culture in the ghettoized society of the United States. We will explore the effects of an imprisoned lifestyle on communities of color and on white communities in the United States. As in previous chapters, we will make a concerted effort to show racism's destructive effects on its perpetuators. Then, as a conclusion to the three chapters that have explored the three primary manifestations of racism within the

United States, we will look briefly beyond the borders of the United States to view the global nature of racism's prison.

The Making of a Monoculture

That which is popularly referred to as "American" culture is, for the most part, an amalgam of European cultures. Our language is from England, our music and literature from all over Europe, our religious and moral values from Judeo-Christian tradition. While our lifestyle has continued to evolve into something called American, it would be more accurately referred to as European American. For, as we shall see, the other four racial/cultural groupings have been prevented from directly participating in the development of our culture. Thus, that which we know as American culture is in fact a monoculture, an offshoot of what is generally referred to as white western culture.

Over the centuries, white western people—primarily Europeans—have developed great art, music, literature, and a variety of other cultural accomplishments. It is an inheritance of richness and beauty. There have, similarly, been great achievements in science, technology, medicine, education, and the humanities. Despite the fact that there have been other highly developed cultures in Asia, Africa, and Central and South America, western society has dominated that which is called "modern civilization."

On the other hand, much in the history of white western culture is horrifying and shameful, not the least of which is the subjugation and exploitation of people from other races and cultures. The myth of white, racial, and cultural superiority has provided the justification for centuries of political, economic, and cultural dominance of the third world. In the United States, it has brought about virtual genocide of Native Americans, enslavement of Africans, and the exploitation and oppression of Hispanic and Asian people as they came to this country.

The Cultural Curtain

When different cultures come into extended contact with each other, a new culture eventually emerges. It is derived from the strongest elements of each, through a turbulent process of cultural interaction, confrontation, and conflict. As the Greeks and the Romans collided, for example, the strongest characteristics of each became a part of the enriched culture.

It is possible, however, through the use of force, to prevent the cultural interaction, confrontation, and conflict that create new expressions of culture, either by keeping neighboring cultures separated or by forced domination of one culture and the suppression or co-opting of cultural achievements of the subjugated groups.

This is what happened in the United States. Interaction among the five racial/cultural groupings was never permitted to happen. An almost impenetrable "cultural curtain" was created to separate the European American culture from African American, Native American, Hispanic, and Asian cultures. This curtain likewise separates and causes hostility among the latter four racial/cultural groupings. As we look more closely at this curtain and its effects, we shall see that in addition to victimizing those who are placed on the outside, it isolates and threatens to destroy the white racial grouping on the inside.

This cultural curtain is clearly evident in our daily lives. The five racial/cultural groups we have identified as part of American society have lived in a state of forced isolation from one another. The dominant white race has continued to define the culture of the United States, while the other four groupings have been permitted neither to mix nor contribute to a new multicultural group.

In the United States, European American people acted swiftly to dominate and separate themselves from the other four racial/cultural groupings. By killing, enslaving, and herding into reservations and into ghettos almost all red, brown, yellow, and black people, the white dominant group prevented virtually all possibility of cultural interaction. United States culture was therefore determined and defined by European Americans. Behind the cultural curtain the life-style, language, art, music, and all other aspects of culture in the United States were developed, without contest, to favor that which was white and western. Dr. William B. McClain of Wesley Theological Seminary writes that instead of cultural pluralism in America, a cultural arrogance developed, and a sad history of subjugating and exploiting persons who are not part of white culture and the white race within the United States has been written. We have missed the opportunity to enjoy the riches which God has so generously invested in human creation.

Our cultural arrogance has left us impoverished. It has also left us with a large group of "unmeltable" ethnics who are on the outside of the culture looking in. How, and on what terms, we shall learn to become one, have become urgently pressing questions.[2]

The Melting Pot

It is popular, but inaccurate, to describe the United States as a cultural melting pot. This image was created during the years of European immigration, and is based solely on the "melting" of white ethnic groups. From the very beginning, as is reflected in the following words of Israel Zangwill, written in 1921, the melting pot became a triumphal image of white racial/cultural superiority:

> America is God's Crucible, the great Melting Pot where all the races of Europe are melting and reforming!—Here you stand, good folk, think I, when I see you at Ellis Island, here you stand, in your fifty groups, with your fifty languages and histories, and your fifty blood hatreds and rivalries. But you won't be long like that, brothers, for these are the fires of God. A fig for your feuds and your vendettas! German and Frenchmen, Irishmen and English, Jews and Russians, into the Crucible with you all. God is making the American!
> . . . The real American has not yet arrived. . . . He will be the fusion of all the races, perhaps the coming superman.
> . . . Ah, what is the glory of Rome and Jerusalem, where all the races come to worship and look back, compared with the glory of America, where all nations come to labour and look forward.[3]

There is a sense in which Zangwill's vision did come true. European cultures have, for the most part, been so melded as to become almost indistinguishable in the mainstream European American culture. But even that limited success is really no success at all. Rather, it is a great loss, culturally speaking. For, the success of the melting pot assumes the destruction of one's own specific cultural heritage.

True multicultural identity is not created in a melting process in which all identification of the prior components is lost. A more acceptable image is a salad bowl of cultures in which all the ingredients retain their identity; or a cultural stew in which the flavors of all the ingredients become intermingled, creating a new flavor, but still retaining the integrity of each ingredient.

In any case, neither the melting pot nor the salad bowl describe accurately what has happened in the United States. Sealed off by the cultural curtain, African Americans, Native Americans, Hispanics, and Asians have never been permitted to contribute to the creation of an American culture.

It is true that there are "borrowings" from other racial and ethnic traditions by European American cultures. There are streets called calles, and cities named San Jose and Tallahassee; Southwestern architecture is heavily influenced by Spain, Mexico, and Asia; the food, clothing, and dance of many nations and cultures have become part of our cultural scene. But the decision to borrow has always been made by the dominant white culture.

Borrowing is far too mild a word to describe the way in which cultural developments from other racial and ethnic groups come into the white community. In white America, many new forms of music, dance, fashion, and language (especially slang) are either directly appropriated or modified from ideas that began in communities of color, primarily the African American community. It is easy to trace directly to their origins in the African American community, such dance forms as the Charleston and the Black Bottom in the 1920s; rock and roll, the twist, and disco; not to mention jazz, blues, and rock. Imitation, it is often said, is the highest form of flattery. But when the imitation is done with neither permission nor acknowledgment, and when it is accompanied by assertions that the culture from which it is taken is inferior, then imitation becomes the lowest form of racist theft. People of color have a saying that helps to express their anger about the myth of the melting pot: "When you use a melting pot, that which is on the bottom gets burnt, and the scum rises to the top."

Integration: Another Word for Assimilation

Cultural interaction between whites and other racial/cultural communities in the United States is largely prevented by keeping people separated by this cultural curtain, and by carefully selecting and often renaming those elements of their culture that are permitted to slip through. Another method of controlling cultural interaction is to permit the entry of small numbers of people of color into the dominant culture, but only through assimilation and acculturalization. If Native Americans, African Americans, Asians, or Hispanics are willing to forfeit their language, heritage, values, and other aspects of their racial/cultural identity and become "Americanized," they may find it less difficult to slip through the cultural curtain. Unfortunately, this is usually what is meant by the goals of racial "integration." White communities have been willing, gradually and in token measure, to integrate their neighborhoods and schools, as long as it does not change the way they live.

Many white people are shocked when people of color resist integration and assimilation and instead become increasingly conscious and proud of their own culture identities. More and more, people of color are seeking to rediscover and retain their cultural identity and to demand that it be recognized as part of the cultural identity of the United States. The editors of *Sojourner* magazine write as follows:

> The questioning of integration as social policy, and the resultant exploration of new models and definitions of racial identity and progress, has been simmering in the black community for years. The ramifications of this discussion will potentially impact every American, as it calls into question some of the most fundamental assumptions about the ordering of a pluralistic society.[4]

A truly American culture, if it is permitted to develop in the United States, will be a multicultural expression of the Hispanic, African, Asian, European, and Native cultures that already exist in our nation. However, the development of such a multiculture could not happen without the kind of honest cultural interaction that has been described in the previous pages. A multicultural society cannot be based upon the ability of one culture to overpower another. As we move now to a closer look at the dominant white culture, our search must focus on ways to eliminate the cultural curtain and to build bridges between divided cultures.

Life Behind the Cultural Curtain

Outside the cultural curtain, people of color in the United States can point to examples in virtually all areas of their lives of how they are affected by racist exploitation and oppression. Food, clothing, work, language, music, art, sex life, religion, education, and more—life in all its aspects has been determined or heavily influenced by the controlling force of white racism.

Likewise, whether we realize it or not, the list of ways in which the white community has been affected by its life inside the cultural curtain is just as long. Our lifestyle is dramatically affected by white racism. As we shall try to make clear in the following pages, almost everything about our lifestyle would be very different without cultural racism and our retreat behind the cultural curtain. We will use a unique method to explore this thesis. We will look at the kind of sociological language that was originally developed to describe people of color, and then apply it to our own situation. Sociologists have created a special analytical process and vocabulary to describe and define racial problems that are unique to "minority" communities. Once an area or a neighborhood has been identified as a "minority community," it can be examined through the sociologists' "minority community glasses," which make every problem a "racial problem." For example, in any other community a person without a job is simply "unemployed," but an African American or a person who is Hispanic without a job is classified as "minority unemployed." What are simply school problems in any other place become "problems of minority education." Whatever the issue—housing, school, jobs, streetlights, sewers, sex, welfare, family life—in the "minority community," they become racial problems: "Black community housing," "Indian education," "Hispanic unemployment," "Asian community streetlights," "minority sewer problems," "minority sex problems," "minority welfare problems." Categories such as "cultural deprivation," "welfare syndrome," or "familial deterioration" are part of the everyday language to describe people of color in the United States. A totally different vocabulary is used, of course, to describe the white community—a vocabulary that gives more pleasant names to our illnesses. For example, we live in "communities" and "neighborhoods"; they live in "ghettos," "inner cities," and "slums." We have "youth disturbances"; they have "race riots." The use of such sociological languages to describe our separate existences helps to make the cultural curtain even more impenetrable.

The White Racial Ghetto

Now let us reverse the use of this language, using the ghetto terminology to describe life inside the cultural curtain. It will demonstrate that the cultural curtain has harmed not only people of color by locking them out, but has also harmed us by locking us in. It will show that every aspect of our lives has been distorted by our own racial/cultural isolation. Our culture embodies a lifestyle and a set of problems that result directly from our confinement in a prison built by racism. We have been separated by our white identity. The language we speak, the food we eat, the people we marry, the songs we sing, the organizations we belong to are all unique because of our separate residential and cultural life. And they would be very different if we did not live behind a cultural curtain.

Racism causes our separation. Separation causes our racial problems. Because our lifestyle is different, so are the problems related to it. The dilemmas of family life, education, economy, health, and security are direct manifestations of our lifestyles. If there were no racial segregation, we would, of course, still have problems, but they would not be defined in terms of our racial or ethnic identity.

If, behind the cultural curtain, we use this same sociological language to describe our white European American communities, we can learn a great deal about how our isolation has harmed us. When the vocabulary used to analyze other racial and ethnic groups is used to describe the white community, it may even be, ironically, more accurate than when it is applied to communities of color. Such an approach demonstrates with startling clarity that the white community has severe problems as a result of its enslavement to its own racism. Moreover, by using a common language for both communities, the gulf between them might be narrowed.

To begin with, white people, too, live in a "racial ghetto." Although we may have built the walls ourselves, the resulting isolation and its effects are equally harmful. We live in a ghetto, on a reservation, in a separated, cut-off state of existence. We are racially, institutionally, and culturally segregated from people who are not white. Our communities are sterile, homogeneous places of look-alike, dress-alike, act-alike conformity.

As a white racial ghetto, our community can be examined through the same sociological "ghetto lenses" used on the "minority" racial community. Such a conceptual framework immediately turns every problem in our community into a racial problem. If they have "minority racial youth problems," we have "white racial youth problems." If they have minority racial family problems, then we have white racial family problems. Even our environmental issues can be seen as white racial problems. All our problems, lived out in separation, can be related to our white identity and our European American culture. And the names we give to these problems can be the very same names we give to comparable problems that are identified as racial problems in the "minority" ghetto. If the language is accurate to describe those outside the cultural curtain, then it should be just as accurate to describe life on the inside. "Cultural deprivation," for example, might well be an accurate phrase to critique our limited lifestyle. When applied to people of color, the term refers to the fact that they are not able to participate in the richness of our culture.

Cultural deprivation would then be equally an issue in the white community because we are not able to participate in the richness of their cultures. Our communities are separated from each other, and in our separation, we become fearful and hostile. We have different expressions of language, art, music, and literature. We cannot understand each other's artistic concepts of what is good and bad, beautiful and ugly, desirable and undesirable. And in our separation and ignorance, it is a moot question as to who is more or less culturally deprived. Some years ago, John B. Hightower, then director of the New York Museum of Modern Art, wrote in the *Saturday Review* the following words, which are as meaningful today as they were twenty years ago:

> We also hear much about "cultural deprivation," which means, of course, that people in the black and Puerto Rican neighborhoods do not hear white symphonies or see white plays; and it implies that the culture of the ghetto is primitive compared to white culture. Yet the black and ethnic sections of cities are, quite to the contrary, where the arts are most immediate and full of life. If there are any culturally disadvantaged ghettos, they are probably to be found in the white suburbs. . . .
>
> Most of what we count as "culture," in that most ponderous of all possible words, is more European than American. The unmistakable mark of black studies and black arts is their uniquely American quality. . . .
>
> We are being retaught by the ghettos that the arts are about people—the way they see, the sounds they make. It may be that the ghettos will teach us once again how to sing about ourselves in a way that reminds us that the beauty and quality of all our lives and the content of our arts is inseparable.[5]

Our cultural isolation not only prevents us from sharing in the riches of other cultures in the United States; it also drains the excellence from our own cultural expressions, leaving behind an increased blandness and weakness. It takes only one evening of television, or one day in a public school classroom, or a walk through a suburban shopping mall to recognize the deterioration of our values, the insipid nature of much of our self-expression, and the ugliness we often create out of our affluence. Isolated, sterile, and devoid of stimulation behind our cultural curtain, our lives are increasingly flabby, boring, dishonest, and corrupt. One African American observer put it like this: "You white people keep your communities closed because you think a whole lot of us want to come there and live with you. Well, you can relax, because we've been comparing our lifestyles to yours, and frankly, we've decided we like ours better." Who is culturally deprived? "Educational deficiency," another area of minority racial problems identified by sociologists, can also apply to the white community. For decades, educators have measured the inadequacy of schools in communities of color. The average ninth grader in the inner city has a fourth- or fifth-grade reading level. Most nonwhite high school graduates are not academically qualified to enter even the weakest of our colleges. Many educational experts say that four times the current budget is required to reverse the educational deficiencies of children of color. The problems are portrayed as nearly insurmountable, and most remedial programs begin to seem like whitewash to cover a rotten structure.

It is, of course, a glaring reality that, as a result of racism, a decent education in the United States is far more accessible to white people than to people of color. However, educational deficiency is also a problem in the white community. Quality education is simply impossible in a ghetto—any ghetto. Education in a ghetto is a contradiction in terms. No genuine educational process can tolerate isolation and separation. Education by its very nature seeks to expand horizons and rebel against enforced limitation. So long as our separated cultural prisons exist, the only true educational process is one that rebels against the limitations of its setting.

The educational system in our white community presupposes racial segregation as a natural state of existence. It perpetuates the racial prison and enslaves the bodies and minds of children, teaching them to adjust. It does not free people nor does it create conditions within which free people can thrive. A high-quality education must be made as available to people of color as it is to white people. But an education that does not motivate students of any color to break down the racial/cultural curtain is truly a poor education.

A final white racial problem is "familial deterioration." As a sociological category, its application to people of color has always been inaccurate. For example, Native American and African American cultures are based upon an extended family system. Yet, their family issues are measured according to the values of the western nuclear family life. Moreover, the development of a nuclear family among African Americans has always been systematically obstructed by the dominant white culture. In slave days, marriages were rarely permitted, and children were separated from their parents at a very young age. Since reconstruction, the obstacles placed by white society into the paths of African American men have made it very difficult for them to support their families. The greater ease with which women are hired has continued to undermine African American men. And, finally, continuing poverty and slum conditions, including welfare stipulations and many other factors, have continually subverted the stability of the family in African American culture. Thus, it is not the nuclear family model, but the strength of the extended family system among people of color, particularly among African Americans, that has contributed significantly to their ability to survive the ravages of racism. Family deterioration is not an accurate description of the issues surrounding their family life.

However, the concept of familial deterioration certainly is accurate when used to describe the white community. In white western culture, the nuclear family has always been described as the cornerstone of our social structure. *Familial deterioration* is hardly a strong enough term to describe what has been happening in the collapse of the white family, the spiraling divorce rate, and the growing generation gap. Such symptoms have become so severe that one youth worker in a California suburb says he simply assumes that 75 percent of the teenagers have no parents, only an adult stranger or two that they happen to be living with. Who has a racial problem of family deterioration?

Lifting the Cultural Curtain

It is not difficult to dream the dream of a multicultural society in the United States. All the components are there. Each of the five separate cultures exists in an isolated monocultural condition. When the cultural curtain is lifted, all will be able to participate in creating a truly American multicultural society. Each of them will contribute to the formation of an incredibly beautiful cultural rainbow.

The lifting of the cultural curtain need not, indeed must not, be for the purpose of dumping every group into a "melting pot," and creating another monoculture in which the identity of each part is lost. Rather, it must be a "salad bowl" or a "stew" of diverse pluralism without sacrificing each distinct culture. Read once more the words of Dr. William McClain:

> What is the nature of the pluralism we seek? For our purpose here, "pluralism" is used to mean a condition in society in which members of diverse ethnic, racial, religious and social groups maintain autonomous participation in and development of their own traditional culture or specific interests within the confines of a common society and form of government. It means an unwillingness on the part of these ethnic, racial and social groups to sacrifice their own identity, history, ideas, memories, sentiments, aspirations, values and social and cultural styles for the sake of the dominant white, Western European tradition. It does not refer simply to the variety of such things as exotic recipes, colorful costumes, and folk dances (although these may be part of it), but includes interaction among such significant intangibles as values, ways of looking at life and the world, diverse traditions and ideas; the impact that minority groups are having on the redistribution of political power; the extension of civil rights; a different interpretation of history; and the more direct, positive meaning in individuals' lives that results from pluralistic thinking. Pluralism means realizing, affirming and appreciating an extraordinary diversity among us in the same place.[6]

The cultural curtain will not be lifted, at least voluntarily, until there is a deep sense of need within the European American commmunity to come out of its isolation. It will happen only when we become aware of how much we are losing and how much there is to gain from co-participating in the creation of a truly American culture. We have already spoken of "borrowing" what we needed, and quietly slipping it under the curtain, which demonstrates that we do sometimes know a good thing when we see it. However, we must go much further than such questionable "borrowing." The kind of two-way communication and mutual sharing necessary for the creation of a pluralistic society will only happen as a result of true repentence from our cultural arrogance —a conversion experience—and, as Dr. McClain puts it:

> a truly pluralistic theology, a theology that reflects the full range of human experience because it rests not on white experience alone, but on the wider experience of the human race, and includes the contributions of all ethnic groups. To this kind of theology, Benjamin Reist has given the name "pentagular theology," or five-sided theology, because it includes not only white experience, but red, yellow, black and brown experience as well.[7]

Finally, a multiracial and multicultural society will be created only if we expend a greal deal of energy. Lifting the cultural curtain is not easy. It is weighted down with centuries of indoctrination, and lifting it will take the concerted effort of every community and institution in the country. That will be the difficult part. But what follows, even if demanding, will be filled with the joy and excitement of creating a truly American multicultural society.

Conclusion: Racism and Global Reality

In the past three chapters, we have explored the three primary manifestations of racism in the United States: individual, institutional, and cultural. By way of concluding these portrayals, let us briefly look beyond the boundaries of the United States to the reality of global racism. Racial exploitation and oppression of people of color in our own country cannot be fully understood without considering the larger context of white western colonial exploitation and imperialism throughout the world. Let us restate once more our working definition: Racism is the power of one racial group to control and exploit another. And let us remember that to determine whether such power exists we must measure the results. When we contrast the reality of suffering and oppression within most nations in Africa, Asia, and Central and South America with the powerful and privileged lifestyle of most people living in the western nations of Europe and North America, we see that the racism we enforce in the United States exists also as a worldwide reality.

It is not only that individual nations in southern Africa, Central America, the Caribbean, and southeast Asia are embroiled in struggles against racist exploitation by white and western peoples. It is rather that a system of "global apartheid" is rigidly imposed and enforced, dividing the western nations from virtually all of those we call "third-world" countries. Such global apartheid bears all the identifying characteristics of the apartheid system in South Africa, or the system of racism in the United States, and it serves the same purpose: to control and exploit people of color for economic gain. Seeking to analyze this system of global exploitation, a World Council of Churches conference held in the Netherlands in the 1980s made the following statement:

> This [global] system is racist in a variety of ways: it sets the framework for world order based on the values and interests of the white order; it was historically based substantially on the exploitation of the non-white peoples; it projects a continuing and expanding exploitation of the land and resources of the eastern and southern hemispheres—regions where the indigenous people are black, brown, red or yellow. In continuing to strip these people of their resources, this system perpetuates their underdevelopment and frustrates their aspirations for the future.
>
> This system is repugnant to the Christian concept of justice, a denial of the lordship of Christ and therefore an abomination to the Creator.[8]

When racism is viewed on this global level, it is not so easy to separate its institutional and cultural manifestations. From racism's inception in the colonial era and for more than 500 years thereafter, economic exploitation was rationalized with the assumption of cultural superiority on the part of the colonizers, an assumption that gave them what they perceived as the right as well as the responsibility to transform their colonies into cultural images of themselves.

How It Got That Way

In our analysis of racism within the United States, we discovered that the structure and system of racism in our day could be understood only in the light of the deliberate decisions of the past — decisions that provide the foundation for racism even today. The same principle applies to global apartheid. It did not happen recently, nor by accident. Deliberately and historically traceable decisions and actions created the systems that continue to control and exploit the third world to this day. They are so deeply embedded that serious efforts to dismantle them have thus far seemed to make the situation even more difficult.

Beginning with Africa in the fifteenth century, each continent of the third world was conquered and subdivided. Then the colonizing nations, either by warfare with one another or by amicable agreement, designated the people and property of each colony as "belonging to" them. Gradually, indigenous people and cultures were destroyed or subjugated. The culture of the colonizing nation, as well as its political and economic structures, were imposed in such ways as to create a permanent relationship of dependency that lasted long after official independence, and in many cases to this very day.

How It Stayed That Way

Until 1945, 99.5 percent of what we now call the third world was under western domination. Then, from 1945 to 1970, an amazing thing happened. In what historian Ralph Winter calls "twenty-five unbelievable years" in his book by the same title, this figure was reversed. In 1969, 99.5 percent of the third world's colonies had become politically independent. Only a few countries, such as Rhodesia and Vietnam, and a few islands in the Pacific and the Caribbean still remained the property of colonizers.

However, it became quickly apparent that the end of western colonies did not eliminate western control over these areas. In some ways, decolonization actually paved the way for greater control and greater exploitation through economic and cultural imperialism. Granting political independence to the colonies of Europe and America was not usually a voluntary action resulting from kindness and respect, nor did it indicate a willingness to relinquish control. Rather, it was a response to the recognition that control could no longer be maintained in such directly oppressive ways. New forms of control were immediately substituted. Just as the conscious and direct forms of institutional racism in the United States were supplanted by more easily hidden indirect forms of racism, so also the control of the non-Western world continued indirectly, even though formal colonization had nearly ceased to exist. Ralph Winter continues the story:

> A factor tending to counterbalance the withdrawal of political imperialism was a heightened economic imperialism. The impinging of western industrial and business enterprises upon the non-western people generally increased. . . . Indeed, in some cases the withdrawal of the colonial governments gave a freer rein to western business enterprises than was the case prior to independence. Sometimes a new national government was less able or less willing to protect certain elements of the population than was the former colonial government. Thus, a kind of economic imperialism continued despite the decrease in political imperialism.
>
> In view of this complexity, it is not surprising to note that there was a lingering, indeed increasing, cultural imperialism. . . . Continuing economic imperialism brought a continuing flood of foreign merchandise, periodicals, and related customs. In an attempt to feel equal to the former colonial culture, local national governments often dictated crash programs of face-lifting cities, new superhighways, western style schools, and even western dress.[9]

Today, the devastating effects of global white racism not only continue to threaten the existence of the third world, but of ourselves in the first and second worlds as well. The twin evils of militarization and overconsumption of resources provide the clearest illustration of this exploitative relationship that threatens to destroy us all.

Even with the welcome reduction of military tension between the United States and the Soviet Union, we are no less threatened by nuclear armaments. It was never simply the possibility of nuclear aggression between the superpowers that comprised the major threat from militarization. For centuries the nations of the West have justified military aggression against the third world on the basis of "national self interest" and "manifest destiny." The continuing struggle in the world is between the haves and the have-nots. A small percentage of the world's population controls and consumes the majority of the world's goods and prevents the majority from having an equal share. United States policy goals for maintaining this present world order are essentially the same today as those stated in 1948 by George Kennan, who at the time headed the State Department planning staff:

> We have about 50% of the world's wealth, but only 6.3% of its populations. . . . In this situation, we cannot fail to be the object of envy and resentment. Our real task in the coming period is to devise a pattern of relationships which will permit us to maintain this position of disparity without positive detriment to our national security. To do so we have to dispense with all sentimentality and day-dreaming; and our attention will have to be concentrated everywhere on our immediate national objectives. We need not deceive ourselves that we can afford today the luxury of altruism and world-benefaction. . . . We should cease to talk about vague and . . . unreal objectives such as human rights, the raising of the living standards and democratization. The day is not far off when we are going to have to deal in straight power concepts. The less we are hampered by idealistic slogans, the better. . . .[10]

Today, the aggression against the third world is more widespread than ever. In the Near and Far East, in Central and South America, and in Africa, through both direct military invasion and through arming of others to fight our wars for us, we continue to destroy the world. We are either unwilling or unable to stop. A term currently used to describe United States strategy to oppose third-world liberation struggles is "low-intensity conflict." Jack Nelson Pallmeyer, an analyst of United States foreign policy, writes the following:

> Low-intensity conflict is the present-day means through which the United States seeks to achieve generally unstated foreign-policy goals in the third world. . . .

The victims of low-intensity conflict are not limited to the poor. Also at stake is the future of our own democracy and the integrity of our faith. Low-intensity conflict is so broad in scope, so cynical in outlook, so damaging in practice that it presents Christians and churches in the United States with a situation similar to that faced by the Confessing churches in Nazi Germany. In short, low-intensity conflict presents us with a confessional situation that demands acknowledgement of our participation in a sinful situation, repentence and creative action.[11]

That which is not destroyed by military aggression, we consume. For years, we have been recklessly misusing the world's resources in an insane attempt to satisfy our appetite for material goods. Consider the appalling fact that two thirds of the world's people are poverty-stricken, most of them nonwhite. While they starve, over 50 percent of the goods produced throughout the world each year is consumed in the United States. The pollution of air, land, and water, and other disturbances of the ecological balance have now brought us and the rest of the world to a point of crisis. There can be no escape from the reality that this crisis of destruction and consumption is a direct result of racist domination by the white western world.

New Global Changes: Signs of Hope?

Alongside this terribly depressing picture of global apartheid and continuing indirect colonial aggression, there have been some new and seemingly positive events. During the past few years we have seen amazing changes in the world. This time it is not only the changes of the "third world," but the "second world" of Russia and eastern Europe as well. The collapse of the political and economic structures that held together the Soviet Union's system of satellites in eastern Europe has created waves of change throughout the world. The cold war, at least in its most visible expression, is over. The nose-to-nose confrontation between the first and second worlds, the capitalist and communist worlds, seems to be at an end, at least for the present. This confrontation will, of course, inevitably be replaced by other tensions and conflicts.

Nevertheless, the end of the cold war is a welcome positive achievement.

Simultaneously, exciting political changes are taking place in various parts of the third world. Namibia has achieved independence. The inevitable end of apartheid in South Africa is slowly moving toward fulfillment. Chile has moved once again into a democratic electoral process. The divided Koreas are beginning to resolve their unstable separation. Such situations are always unpredictable, and things will surely change between the time these words are written and the time they are read. Moreover, none of these positive developments can be evaluated without being considered within the context of the increasingly serious global economic situation in which each of these nations is caught.

Unfortunately, the lessening of conflict between the U.S.S.R. and the United States does not necessarily mean a change in the way either country relates to the third world. In some cases, it may even mean an increase in tensions in the third world. During the so-called cold war, a third world nation might have had hostile relations with one superpower, but it would almost automatically have the support of the other. Since there is no longer such competition for loyalty, theoretically at least, there is also no assurance of automatic support.

Perhaps nothing more clearly illustrates these old insecurities in the midst of new hope than the vivid remarks of an African representative to the United Nations. It is said that at a meeting of the General Assembly in celebration of the lessening tensions between the United States and Russia, the delegate took his turn to speak: "My nation also wishes to join the assembly in expressing our delight and gratitude that the tension and conflict is lessening between these two giant nations. As all of you know, my nation and many other tiny nations of the world have felt tossed and turned about, because of the cold war. There is a saying in my country, 'When two elephants fight, it is the grass that suffers.' "

"However," continued the delegate, when the murmurs of agreement had died down, "I also want to express a word of caution, and of the fear among my people that the new friendliness between these two great nations does not necessarily mean an end to our problems. The friendliness between these two giants may be as detrimental to small nations such as ours, as was their hostility. For there is another saying among the people of my country: 'When two elephants make love, the grass still suffers.'

Summary: The Continuing Connections

In this chapter we have seen that racism's destructive forces have affected almost every aspect of the culture and lifestyle of everyone living in the United States. It is also clear that the cultural curtain that divides us must be lifted before we can create a truly multicultural society. Finally, the dismantling of deeply rooted racism in our own country is not possible without an acute awareness of its interconnectedness with the "global apartheid" by which white racism dominates and exploits the third world.

While the purpose of this book is to address the issue of racism and racial justice within the United States, we would be greatly deficient in our understanding if we did not recognize this connection between racism in the United States and what we have called "global apartheid": the linkage between the people of our inner cities and reservations with the people of the third world. It is also critically important to be sensitive to these connections and how they affect our efforts to combat and eradicate racism here at home.

6

WHITE RACISM AND THE CHURCH

Both oppressor and oppressed seek religious legitimation. Both sides invoke the name of God and Jesus Christ, and Christians are found on both sides of the political conflict. . . . Nor does the matter end there. The political conflict has now entered into the churches. The church has become a site of struggle.
—from **The Road to Damascus: Kairos and Conversion,** *a document by Christians from seven third-world nations*

There is no clearer vision of racial justice and equality than that which is given in the Bible. This vision is an invincible weapon for combating racism and a powerful tool for the building of a multiracial and multicultural society. It provides a clear understanding that the whole human family is created by God to exist in unity and equality, and a clear judgment that any violation of God's intentions, including racism, is a sin against both God and humanity. Even more important is the message of God's intervention and redemption, with an invitation and a command to repent of our divisions, to be forgiven, restored, and empowered to rebuild God's human family on the basis of unity, love, and justice.

With this vision and with this commission we are empowered to overcome racism and to build a racially just society.

The terrible tragedy is that these teachings of the Bible and the church have become distorted and are made to serve demonic purposes. Not only have the church's teachings been compromised, but the church itself has become a part of the prison of racism, its leadership co-opted into assisting the warden and the guards. The historical fact is that the church has often blessed deliberate acts of direct racism. The church, together with other institutions in contemporary society, remains captive to the continued systemic racism of the present and is to a great extent still unrepentent for it.

Most of us are horrified by the distortions of Christianity taught by white supremacist organizations and other right-wing fundamentalists. Their misuse of God's name to defend hatred and exploitation appalls us. But the responsibility for this misuse does not lie only with those who openly sow the seeds of racial hatred. To our great shame, our own mainline churches have all too often allowed themselves to be identified with racial supremacists. And when the times called for forceful and courageous proclamation of the truth based on clear biblical understanding, our churches, and we ourselves, have often turned aside because of internal pressures and political expediency. This unfaithfulness has resulted in continued confusion about the content of Scripture and Christian teaching, as well as the scandalous reality that the church today is still the most racially segregated institution in the United States.

At the same time, the marvelous contrasting reality is that the message of the Christian faith has given millions of exploited and oppressed people the strength to struggle for survival, to have hope, and to fight for their own liberation. Likewise, some of the most courageous and brilliant leaders in the struggle for racial justice have come from the church. Often their campaigns for freedom are opposed by other Christians. Often they are rejected by the "official" church, as were Jesus and the prophets. But their strength and determination are witness to the power of the Christian message, even if that message is also twisted and confused by others who claim to be its legitimate guardians.

This contradiction between our high expectations of the church, on one hand, and our great disappointment in many of its deeds, on the other, must be faced with honesty and realism. Like each of us, the church is, in the language of the Reformation, *simul justis et peccator,* simultaneously holy and sinful. The church is both divine instrument of God and human institution. The church is a part of the Happiness Machine in our fable. But at the same time it is a major force in working for the dismantling of the machine and in writing a just ending to the story.

The goal of this chapter is to apply our analysis of racism to the mainstream, predominantly white church in the United States. First, we will explore some ways in which racism distorts our understanding of the Bible. Second, we will see how it has affected the history of the Christian church. Finally, we will apply our analysis of individual, institutional, and cultural racism to the church as we experience it today.

The Bible and Racism

Let us begin with the Bible. The fundamental, overarching message of the Bible is its emphasis on God's gift of justice and righteousness, of unity and community for all people. The human family is first and foremost the family of God. Racism and racial superiority are contradictory to all the fundamental bibical teachings and cannot be defended on the basis of Scripture. They are neither taught nor implied anywhere in the Bible.

Yet Scripture has repeatedly been misused and distorted to support the forces of racism. Those who seek to sow hatred and division among the races depict the God of the Old and New Testaments as the author of racial superiority and the architect of racial separation. Perhaps the most familiar example is the "curse of Ham." This story in Genesis is misrepresented as an eternal curse of God on all African people.[1] Another example is the misuse of the concept of the "chosen people." In a blasphemous act of self-glorification, colonizers, imperialists, and enslavers take the biblical image of Israel as a chosen people of God and appropriate it for themselves as justification for their actions. A third example is the belief that riches and power are signs of God's blessing. This notion is not only promoted by a great many right-wing sects, but is frequently endorsed both by the traditional churches to explain the riches and power of the United States and the white western world.

It is not within the scope of this book to study any of these misconceptions in great detail. But it is important that we explore why so many people believe these distortions of the Bible. Part of the explanation is, as has often been said, that anyone can read anything into the Bible. Its major themes are, of course, quite clear: creation, sin, redemption, the new realm of love and justice. These central teachings are not easy to distort. But the Bible does not present these ideas in isolated purity. Rather, they are interwoven with stories that are very human and not always clear—stories covering the span of centuries and encapsulated in the frailty of changing language and culture. Often, events and practices contrary to the Bible's main themes of love and justice are recorded without clearly naming them as evil or sinful. Sometimes the biblical writers seem to be supporting and endorsing actions that are contrary to the Bible's strongest principles. War, slavery, polygamy, and prostitution are all at one time or another practiced by the people of God. At times, they even seem to be endorsed by God. A reader of the Bible requires guidance from the best Biblical scholars to work through this maze and to distinguish between that which is presented as divine teaching and that which is discarded along the way as false.

This, however, is not the main difficulty. The real problem is with those who approach the Bible with the deliberate intention of using it to bolster their own racist beliefs. They do this by taking portions of Scripture out of context and distorting them. It is important to understand that people who use the Scriptures to justify racist beliefs do not get their ideas from the Bible. They develop those ideas elsewhere, and interpret the Bible in ways that reinforce them.

There is no denying that the Bible can at times seem confusing. It is true that careful study is required, with the help of biblical scholars, to understand such stories as the curse of Ham or such concepts as the "chosen people." But it is also true that objective study of Scripture reveals that the Bible does not support racial superiority. It is likewise true—and sad—that those who use the Bible to justify racism will not be dissuaded by arguments about such disputed biblical texts.

Thus, it is very important that we not be defensive about the Bible, trying to prove, verse by verse, that those who use Scripture as a basis for racism are wrong. Rather than approaching the Bible in piecemeal fashion, it is far better to view it as a whole, from beginning to end, in terms of its central message: that God has created and redeemed all humankind and all living things to be loved and to love each other in justice and equality. Everything else in the Bible is a historical record of the people of God as they struggle to understand this message and come to terms with it in their own lives. Similarly, our chief purpose in studying the Bible is this same effort to understand its central message and come to terms with it in our own lives.

Racism in the New Testament Church

The first significant theological issue faced by the New Testament church was the issue of racial and cultural inclusiveness. An intense struggle in the early church—a theological debate and a political fight—profoundly affected the beliefs and practices of this new faith. The results of that struggle helped define the content, theology, and organizational direction of the early church. And it still provides inspiration and guidance for us in a struggle that not just resembles the one in the New Testament church but is a continuation of it.

The first Christians were Jews who believed that Jesus was the promised Messiah. Even though there were people among the followers of Jesus who were not Jews, the church began as an exclusive Jewish sect with no intention of allowing Gentiles to be members. Soon, however, a number of Gentiles began to adopt the new religion. As the book of Acts and the letters of St. Paul reveal, the early church leaders had to face two difficult questions in rapid succession: first, whether Gentiles could be Christians at all; and second, if so, whether they should be allowed to share equally in the life of the church.[2]

The first question—whether Gentiles could be Christians —was an issue of racial "purity." There was an effort to keep the church "pure," which meant that the church was to be for Jews only and that Gentiles were to be excluded from the fellowship of believers. The battle was over before any significant or long-term damage had been done. It was short because it was impossible to keep the Gentiles from believing in Jesus. If they hadn't been allowed in the Jewish Christians' church, they would inevitably have started a church of their own. It was clearly impossible to build a fence around this global, universal faith and to reserve it for a limited audience.

In the tenth chapter of Acts, we read that Peter learns in a vision that God doesn't make distinctions in the creation between clean and unclean. Then, in an encounter with the gentile centurion Cornelius, Peter realizes that the meaning of his vision was that all people, including those whom the Jews considered "unclean," were to be included in the new church. Soon after, at the first church council meeting in Jerusalem, a decision was made that set the stage for the swift missionary expansion of the church. The decision was that God's reconciling grace and forgiveness as revealed in the gospel are for everyone. The church was to be radically and unconditionally inclusive. The following are quotes from that decision, as well as from later interpretations of the decison, in a sermon by St. Paul:

> Everyone who believes in him receives forgiveness of sins through his name. (Acts 10:43)

> If then God gave them the same gift that he gave us when we believed in the Lord Jesus Christ, who was I that I could hinder God? (Acts 11:17)

> Everyone who believes is set free from all those sins from which you could not be freed by the law of Moses. (Acts 13:39)

But the issue was still not fully resolved. More trouble was on the horizon. Simply making the decision against the "purists" and in favor of full acceptance of everyone into the church did not end the problem. The question of inclusiveness escalated into a second and far more complicated issue. Once the decision was made that God does not exclude anyone from the church, the conflict evolved into a power struggle for control of the church, a battle by the church's charter members to maintain power over the newcomers. Those who had wanted to keep the Gentiles out of the church now wanted to control their lives within the church. They insisted that Gentiles become Jews in order to become Christians.

According to the Jewish leaders of the church, Gentiles would have to be circumcised. They would also have to follow all the traditional laws regulating diet and other aspects of lifestyle. They would have to reject their past cultural identity and assume the identity of a Jew.

Our mothers and fathers in the early church resolved this second issue with the same indisputable clarity as they did the first. After lengthy discussion and debate, it was ruled that Gentiles need not first become Jews in order to be Christians. This decision was made at the second meeting of the church council in Jerusalem. The theological basis for the first decision had been the radical, unconditional acceptance by God of all humankind. No one was to be excluded from the church because of race, culture, gender, or nationality. The second decision added a crucial corollary: Within the church, no race, culture, gender, or nationality was to have superiority or dominance, nor could one group determine the behavior for any other group.

Before we explore how the issue of inclusiveness in the early church applies to our situation today, it must be emphasized that the solution to these issues in the New Testament church did not come easily. The debates were long and difficult, arousing deep feelings that were often filled with great anger. Moreover, although the decisions were made on paper, their implementation was not so simple. The power struggle between the Jews and the Gentiles continued for a very long time.

A final word about these decisions: They were made for all time. No one can change their results. Nevertheless, the church in every age and place has had to face these issues and decide whether or not to implement the decisions of these early Christians. Again and again, the principle has been tested against powerful factions who have attempted to exclude one or another "undesirable" group from the church. Each time, but not without terrible pain and struggle, the church has agreed with St. Paul that "there is no longer Jew or Greek, there is no longer slave or free, male or female; for all of you are one in Christ Jesus" (Galatians 3:28).

Same Scene, Contemporary Setting

These two issues of racial purity and racial dominance faced by the New Testament church are precisely the problems in our own struggle today. A great many people in the church are still fighting the first issue of that New Testament conflict; they are still caught up in a "struggle for racial purity," believing themselves to be clean and acceptable, while others are not. That, for example, is the nature of the struggle in South Africa. It is also the primary issue of the Ku Klux Klan, as its members seek to portray themselves as superior people. But, lest we be tempted to portray ourselves as superior to the Ku Klux Klan, we need to recognize how deeply the belief in racial superiority is still lodged in our hearts.

For the most part, however, the churches have made their decision about this first issue. Today few churches in our society would disagree that their doors should be open to all, regardless of race, culture, gender, or nationality. It should, of course, never have been an issue in the first place, and the decision was far too long in coming. In the New Testament church, it was made quickly, so that the Gentiles never needed seriously to consider the founding of a separate gentile church. In the case of the United States churches, the decision took more than 300 years, so that it became necessary for people of color to develop their own churches. These churches have become powerfully important in their lives. Because we waited so long to resolve the first issue, the tragic existence of separate Christian denominations on the basis of race will now take many years to undo.

Nevertheless, like the New Testament church, we have moved from the struggle for racial inclusiveness to the second issue. Our question is no longer whether we will exclude but how we will include others in the church. And, like the New Testament church, the main issue is who will define and control the process of becoming racially inclusive.

For the early church, this question of control was expressed in the following way: Must Gentiles first become Jews in order to become Christians? Today, the same question is expressed in a similar way: Do persons of other races and cultures need first to become like European Americans in order to become Christian? Is it not like insisting on circumcision to expect African Americans, Asians, Native Americans, and Hispanics to become culturally and religiously like European Americans in order to be a part of our congregations? And is that not a perpetuation of the same struggle to maintain power and control of the church?

The above questions can be directed to a congregation in the first stage of opening its doors, waiting for the first person of color to walk into the church. Or they can be directed to a congregation that already has a significant number of people of color in its membership and is being challenged to reflect its racial and cultural diversity in worship and other areas of congregational life. The same questions can be used to look at an entire denomination that might be exploring new educational models to prepare people of color for the ministry. Conversely, they can be addressed to a denomination that is discovering the need to provide education and training for its white members so that they will better understand inclusiveness and diversity in the life of the church. In each case we deal with exactly the issue that was faced by the New Testament church: Who will define and who will control the church as it seeks to be radically and unconditionally inclusive of all God's people? Just as the solutions to these issues dramatically affected the life of the church in the first century, so also will our solutions significantly influence the Christian church of the twenty-first century.

A History of Two Churches

We turn now from the Bible and the early church to a brief look at the issue of racial inclusiveness in the church's 2,000-year history. We begin with the realization that the Christian church has always been somewhat schizophrenic. On the one side it is strong, successful, and confident to the point of brashness and arrogance. It identifies comfortably with the rich and powerful, with rulers and generals. It holds the poor and rejected of the world at a distance, yet places a high priority on works of charity and social service. It emphasizes a "theology of glory" or "triumphal theology."

The other side of the church seems weak, unsuccessful, and somewhat antisocial. It befriends the poor, the suffering, and those rejected by the world. It relates to the rich and powerful from a distance and often with a sense of prophetic anger and judgment. It emphasizes a "theology of the cross" or "servant theology."[3]

At the root of these divergent personalities are the same tensions that we have already seen in the New Testament church. The strong, successful church with its theology of glory leans toward exclusiveness, the "superior" races, the "better" classes and the "proudest" nations. In the other church with its theology of the cross one finds the opposite—a tendency toward radical and unconditional inclusiveness and a preference for those who are rejected by the world.

In the following historical summary, we will briefly trace the church's history as "triumphal church" and "servant church." While the reader may feel a closer identity with the servant church, we need to recognize a legitimate place in the church for glory and triumph. The message of the resurrection—God's victory over death—and promise of a triumphal second coming of Christ give the church and individual Christians a sense of hope and confidence that the future belongs to God. Nevertheless, those who identify with the servant church and a theology of the cross contend that the triumphant church all too quickly becomes the "triumphalistic church," placing its confidence in humans (especially governments and rulers), rather than in God, and turning its back on those with whom Christ shared the fate of rejection and suffering.

Historically, the New Testament church began as an illegal and persecuted religion. Thus, it had little difficulty at first in rejecting a triumphalistic identity. In its early life, the church developed deep roots with the rejected, the poor, and the suffering.

Then came success, with all its attendant dangers and terrible choices. In 313 A.D., the Christian church became the official national religion. Constantine, the reigning Roman monarch who gave the church its first official seal of approval, transformed the sign of the cross into an emblem of military conquest. The servant church gave way to the triumphal church as the popular image of Christianity.

In the centuries that followed, the church continued to be pulled in two directions. Its strongest and most visible path was its triumphal identification with the state. The crusades and holy wars, fought in the name of and for the sake of Jesus, expanded the dominion of the church and culminated in the establishment of the Holy Roman Empire. The church and the state became indistinguishable.

At the same time, the servant church followed a less visible, narrower, and seemingly weaker path, the path of identification with the way of the poor and the way of the cross. This path was followed by many religious orders of monks and nuns, who kept alive the image and work of a servant church. Meanwhile, the millions of adherents to Christianity were mostly peasants who, although they may have resembled the monks and nuns in their lifestyle of poverty, did not choose it voluntarily. Moreover, they were scarcely aware of their identification with the servant church, for they gave their loyalty to the triumphal church and state, which in return gave them work, paid their meager salaries, and forgave their sins on Sunday morning.

The Two Churches in the Reformation

The Reformation began with a head-on collision between the triumphal church and a number of forces for change. This collision dramatically changed the face of Christianity. For a brief moment, the world was given its first full exposure to the servant church since Constantine adopted the church as a child of the nation. Among the Reformation's gifts was Luther's immensely important theology of the cross, which has become part of the great heritage of the servant church. Douglas John Hall, a leading authority on Luther's theology of the cross, writes:

> Over against a "theology of glory" which is inherently at-
> tracted to empire, like to like, the "theology of the cross,"
> being translated, is always about God's abiding commitment
> to the world.[4]

To the disappointment of many, however, the Reformation did not establish a Protestant servant church to counter the
triumphal Roman Catholic church. Charles Villa-Vicencio, a
South African theologian, writes:

> Whatever the fundamental cause of these reform processes
> (economic, the rise of nationalism and/or the spiritual re-
> newal) the consequence was the emergence of a bourgeois
> church. The control of the church, and more particularly the
> Protestant church, had shifted from the imperial aristocracy
> to the bourgeois princes, but the peasants continued to be
> marginalized and excluded from the socio-political identity
> of the church.[5]

Thus, it was not long before the church took on a more
triumphal identity than ever. The world was soon to see Protestant state churches providing the blessings of God upon the new
children of enlightenment—the industrial revolution and the capitalist economic system. Moreover, with tirades against the Jews
and the Turks, the Reformation inadvertently built into the foundations of the newly formed Protestant church the ideological basis for the nationalist and racist excesses in Europe and in the
United States that were yet to come. This was perhaps the Reformation's most tragic contribution to contemporary history.

The Two Churches in the New World

About the time of the Reformation, another historic development
called for the direct involvement of both the servant church and
the triumphal church. The "new world" was discovered and being explored, marking the beginning of Europe's colonial conquest of Africa, the Americas, and Asia. Both servant church and
triumphal church boarded the colonial ships and emigrated to the
"new" world. The triumphal church took the high road to which

it was accustomed. It rode in first-class cabins with royal representatives and military leaders. The servant church rode in steerage, together with the servants, vassals, and slaves. Immediately upon landing on foreign shores, representatives of the triumphal church blessed the newly established colonies, and the cross became the sign of the new religion imposed on those who were being colonized. Meanwhile, the servant church also found a new home—with the indentured servants, imported slaves, and colonized peasants.

History books describing the age of discovery and colonialization usually refer only to the triumphal church. The role of the servant church is not widely known: its efforts to provide the oppressed and suffering with spiritual strength to survive; its vision of freedom; its nurturing in the oppressed a spirit of rebellion. In all of these activities, the servant church not only helped keep hope alive but also planted the seeds for many of today's third-world liberation movements. Villa-Vicencio describes further how the church is pulled in two directions to this very day:

> Since those heady days of missionary triumphalism this distinction between two different kinds of political involvement has left an indelible mark on the church. Confessing Christians in Nazi Germany were condemned by church and state alike for resisting Hitler, while the involvement of the Dèutsche Christen on the side of Hitler was regarded as theologically legitimate. In Smith's Rhodesia the church vacillated in its affirmation of social justice, in Latin and Central American dictatorships the institutional churches have in many instances preached an ethereal spirituality that has left the poor to die in the streets, and in the Philippines, South Korea and elsewhere, bishops, priests, nuns, and catechists have been tortured and assassinated by rulers who regard themselves as Christians. In South Africa . . . even the most "liberal" churches question the more radical involvement of Christians against the state.[6]

The Two Churches in the United States

Crispus Attucks was the first American to die in the Revolutionary War that gave the American people their freedom. But the colonies' victory in that war did not set Attucks's people free, for he was an African American. Although the question of white freedom was settled in 1776, slavery was established long before as a foundation stone of the United States' economic system. And the frontier expansion which began shortly thereafter, with its movement westward toward land and gold, resulted in the virtual genocide of an indigenous people.

The path of pride and glory and the path of pain and shame together form the history of the United States; through it all, every step of the way, the church was there as chaplain, priest, prophet. The immigrant church from Europe quickly became rooted in the new nation. While it helped create the unity and union of the Republic, it also suffered many internal divisions, standing on both sides of every significant issue: for and against slavery, for and against emancipation, for and against U.S. imperialism, for and against civil rights, for and against a new multiracial/multicultural identity. But it was its stand on the side of slavery that gave the American church its most persistent and shameful marks of division. Historian and writer C. Eric Lincoln, who is especially insightful about the role of the African American church, addresses himself to the tragic failures of the white church during those years:

> There was a fleeting moment in our history when some denominations sought to commit their churches to do what our Founding Fathers had elected not to do; namely, to give de facto recognition to the principle that all men stand before God equal in their nakedness and need. But in the end the churches failed to rescue what the statesmen decided to overlook. Bigotry seeped through the restraints of faith to join the undertow already sucking at the political foundations of the new nation. Black Christians, despairing of the peculiar spiritual mentality which confined them to the back pews and "nigger heavens" in the white churches, eventually withdrew and founded independent communions.

> If there had been no racism in America, there would be no racial churches. As it is, we have white churches and black churches; white denominations and black denominations; American Christianity and black religion.[7]

Thus it is that both personalities of the church—the triumphal and the servant church—have become an indelible part of the United States. The triumphal church is a largely white nationalistic church, a new American religion with Christianity's familiar characteristics but also in many ways a stranger to biblical Christianity. It is a religion of "holy nationalism" that is, while most clearly expressed in right-wing religious groups, also deeply integrated into the lives of the traditional churches. Like the triumphal church throughout history, today's triumphal church has a nationalist fervor and patriotism, and identifies most strongly with riches and power, but it is not without a patronizing charity toward the poor and needy. This triumphal religion requires an American flag in each of its expansive and expensive sanctuaries, from which triumphal music of trumpet and organ can be heard during Sunday worship. It has contributed at least two new religious holidays: the fourth of July and Thanksgiving Day. It offers prayers at the opening of daily sessions of Congress, at presidential prayer breakfasts, and at luncheon meetings of Lions and Kiwanis clubs throughout the country. Its prayers offer profound thanks to God for the great and prosperous nation we have become and ask for the courage and strength necessary to defend our freedom against all our enemies.

The servant church in the United States, as expected, has been less assuming in its presence and far more modest in its self-appraisal. From its ramshackle churches and storefront buildings one often hears a different kind of music—the plaintive cry of the gospel song and spiritual. Its message has provided a counterpoint to the self-righteousness of the triumphal church. It speaks of pain, suffering, and powerlessness and prays for forgiveness, protection, and release. The servant church has had little power in the secular sense; it has not sought and has seldom received national recognition. At times, however, its voice has been filled with prophetic anger, demanding justice for the oppressed. At such times, the servant church is heard by and receives at least token recognition from the highest offices of the land.

From one perspective, it seems as if the American experience has forced the triumphal church and the servant church farther apart than ever, drawing severe lines and clear distinctions between them. The triumphal church seems mostly white, mostly middle and upper class, mostly in the northern suburbs and traditional rural farming areas of the South and Midwest. The servant church seems to be more often than not among the poor, composed predominantly of people of color, located mostly in the inner cities of the North and West, and rural poverty areas of the South. But things are never quite as they seem. If we look more closely at the predominantly white European American churches, the clear distinction between triumphal church and servant church quickly blurs. Side by side, within each of the many denominations and individual congregations that exist throughout the country, triumphal church and servant church thoroughly intermingle and often are indistinguishable from one another. The theology of glory and its ever-present holy nationalism is not the exclusive property of right-wing sect groups but is a part of all the major denominations. However, neither is the theology of the cross, with its passion for justice, only to be found in the African American, Hispanic, Asian, and Native American churches. It is also an integral part of the predominantly white European American church.

As we turn now to take a closer look at these predominantly white European American churches, we will find in each one a mixture of beliefs and practices, ranging from the most conservative triumphalism to the most radical tenets of servanthood. What these churches all have in commmon, however, is their confinement in a segregated prison of racism. They all worship and live their daily lives in virtual separation from sisters and brothers in the faith who are of another race or ethnic background. Just as the Kerner Report identifies "two societies, black and white," so also must we describe "two churches, black and white." The wall of racism that divides these two churches and keeps them apart has been built by the triumphal church, while the task of tearing it down is the passionate commitment of the servant church.

White Church: White Power, White Prison

We are driving down a suburban street, past rows of ranch-style houses with well-groomed expansive lawns and gardens. At an intersection, we turn into the parking lot of a large church. Before us stands a handsome complex of buildings, and at the center an imposing sanctuary. It is a large, successful, mainline, predominantly white Protestant church. We cross the parking lot and walk toward the church's entrance. The reason for our visit is to explore and improve our understanding of this church's imprisonment in and support of America's system of racism.

As we approach our task, it is important to recognize that this church, together with other congregations of most major denominations, is no stranger to efforts to combat racism and work for racial justice. Some denominations, for example, have programs to combat racism. Some have specific goals for multicultural development in the faith and life of their denomination. At least one large denomination has placed rules for inclusive representation into its constitution.[8] It is the intent of this book to be supportive of these efforts, while at the same time encouraging these religious institutions to be even more aware of the depth and scope of their imprisonment.

As we enter the church let us remind ourselves of several principles regarding racism that we arrived at earlier in this book. First, the racism we seek to identify in this well-to-do and largely European American church is not personal prejudice and bigotry dressed up in Sunday clothes. Our definition of racism is based not on the existence of prejudice and bigotry, but on the power that enforces such bigotry and gives one group the ability to control the other. Our goal in visiting this suburban congregation is to discover specific ways in which the European American church wittingly or unwittingly contributes to this transformation of white prejudice into white power, both in the larger society and the church itself.

A single Christian or even a single congregation may not feel very powerful, but the collective power of the European American church and its various denominations is important in the lives of millions of Christians and exerts significant influence on the decisions and actions of our society. This is true of many issues, including racial justice. The decisions and actions of these institutional churches concerning race have a profound effect both on white Christians and Christians of color.

Second, we need to remember that racism is a prison for its white perpetuators as well as its victims. Long after the deliberate and historically traceable decisions were made that created the predominantly white church in a predominantly white society, and long after the church first began to express its desire to help undo the effects of racial separation and isolation, the marks of its imprisonment in racism remain clearly visible. They manifest themselves in the church's inability to express itself as an inclusive unified people of God. The marks of its imprisonment are evident in the reality that in most congregations it is difficult, often impossible, to talk about racism and issues of racial justice, either as subjects for biblical and theological reflection or as matters of social concern. The marks of its imprisonment are most clearly seen, however, in the comfortable, generally unquestioning way that the European American congregations exist as white ghettoized churches in white ghettoized neighborhoods, locked in the same prison as the other institutions we have been describing.

Third, we need to remember that in measuring the existence of racism in the church it is the results that count. This is as important in defining and discovering racism in the church as in any other institution. The church has always sought to inspire intentions, as well as develop laws and rules, and express principles that give direction to its members. Ultimately, however, the measurement must be whether good intentions and carefully drawn rules result in a church that lives out with measurable results its beliefs about the wholeness and unity of the body of Christ.

Finally, as we enter the narthex of this church, let us remember our conviction that change is possible and that the walls of racism can be made to fall. This certainty is rooted in our faith in the living God of the church we have just entered, the God whose liberating promises we share with Christians of all races and cultures throughout the world. This certainty is also rooted in the awareness that millions of committed people throughout the world, Christian and non-Christian alike, are working systematically to take down the wall of racism, brick by brick by brick. With this in mind, let us explore further the life, function, and structure of this church we are visiting, in order to describe and define the larger church's imprisonment in racism.

Individual White Racism in the Church

As we walk through the corridors of this well-designed and comfortable church building, enjoy its friendly and confident staff, and observe its well-functioning programs, we may recognize the kind of luxurious disguise that we described earlier as hiding the bars of the comfortable prison. It is not only its content, but also the manner and style in which Christianity is lived out, that contributes to a deceptive anesthetizing process.

There is, of course, no overt racism here. If there were, we can be sure that the entire congregation would rise as one to condemn it and work to correct it. The anesthesia is far more subtle, for it seeks to create the certainty that because such obvious problems do not exist, racism does not exist here either. Let us look at some examples of how the anesthesia works.

Many of the myths, distortions, and lies about people of color and white people—especially the myth that denies a causal relationship between the affluence in this community and poverty elsewhere—are also perpetuated in the church. This happens, for the most part, unconsciously and unintentionally in ways that make the old distinctions between sins of omission and commission inadequate. It happens primarily because people come to this place for religious sanction. It is the one place in which the false myths that surround and support our lives should be exposed and challenged—from the pulpit, in the classrooms, and in the behavior of the people. All too often, however, they are not. The existence of the wall of racism is seldom addressed. If the contrast between the privilege here and the lack of privilege on the other side of the wall is pointed out at all, it is primarily for the purpose of encouraging donations to charity. The values and the actions of our nation that are in conflict with Christian faith are generally ignored. This silence, this quiet conspiracy, this lack of questioning contribute to the anesthesia, making it possible to deny the prison's existence. And the tragedy is greater here than anywhere else, because it is in the church that we are encouraged to look for—and find—the truth.

One example of the church's unconscious perpetuation of racism is the distorted and inaccurate teaching of its history. Whether in a congregation's Sunday school or in a denominational seminary, the primary emphasis is still focused on the history of the European church, its heroes and heroines, its holidays, and the accomplishments of white Christians. When the church history of other nations, and especially third-world nations, is taught, distortions and misinformation abound, for the premise is generally based on a mission theology that once considered these countries backward, pagan, and uncivilized. In many denominations, efforts have been made to correct some of these distortions. Both text and artwork are, at least to some degree, mindful of other races and ethnic groups. Seminaries usually require at least one core course dealing with multicultural issues. Distressingly, these historical distortions still heavily influence the church. Similarly, the historical contributions of Christians and churches of other races and ethnic groups in the United States are usually ignored or diminished. And the historical role of the European American churches in helping to perpetuate or even to combat racism is seldom, if ever, addressed.

Another example of the church's contribution to this anesthetizing process is the individualism that is generally taught by the church—the popular American belief that personal worth is measured by private initiative and individual achievement. By contrast, the Christian faith is a religion marked primarily by community. As Christians we find our identity, our relationship to God, and a sense of our ability and worth in the context of community. Yet, the American concept of individualism is perpetuated in almost all the churches as a means of defining our relationship with God and affirming the national creed of private initiative.

The church's imprisonment in individualism helps anesthetize us to the effects of racism. The popular perception is that sin, guilt, and forgiveness are limited to what we as individuals do right or wrong. Responsibility for corporate evil is seldom raised in the church, and many people deny that it has anything to do with a Christian understanding of sin. Yet as we have seen, it is impossible to understand the full effects of racism from the limited perspective of individual actions. The prison of racism is a corporate prison. We can neither comprehend nor eradicate it except from a collective perspective. Our Christian understanding of unity as a corporate family of God can contribute greatly in combating and eradicating racism. The false teaching of individualism serves only to solidify and continue racism's power.

A final illustration of ecclesiastical anesthesia is the popular conception, mentioned earlier, that riches and power are signs of God's blessing on those who possess them. Almost every denomination's book of worship, for example, contains prayers with phrases that refer to the "great riches with which God has blessed us as a nation," or which state that "all we possess is from God's loving hands." Such prayers demonstrate how, through prayers, songs, sermons, and other means of teaching, the Christian community has come to accept the belief that we are rich because God has blessed us. The church, at the very least, ought to be a place where one can question such assertions. Many of the world's poor and powerless are convinced, on the basis of their understanding of Christianity, that large portions of our wealth are not God's gifts at all, but products of racism, greed, and global robbery. In our anesthetized condition, however, we are taught that such assertions are absurd; rather than discuss and analyze them, we listen attentively to sermons affirming our belief that the combined efforts of God and our private initiative have gotten us our well-deserved privilege and power.

Becoming Aware of Our Brokenness

Before leaving the subject of individual racism, we must emphasize the crucial role the church can play in helping us to break through our anesthesia. This is probably the church's most important task in dealing with racism. The process we have called "de-anesthetization" is helping people to become aware of their brokenness as a result of racism. It is taking away the insulation factor that stands between us and feelings of pain, separation, and imprisonment; it is offering a new wholeness to those who seek this alternative way of life.

The most important means for breaking through our anesthesia are the Sacraments of Baptism and Holy Communion. In baptism we receive a vision of the whole human family as one, with all the walls that divide us torn down, melted away, gone.

Because of our baptism, writes St. Paul, walls can no longer separate us:

> Neither death, nor life, nor angels, nor rulers, nor things present, nor things to come, nor powers, nor height, nor depth, nor anything else in all creation, will be able to separate us from the love of God in Christ Jesus our Lord. (Romans 8:38-39)

The baptized Christian who has entered into the community of "unconditional inclusiveness" is committed to a lifelong battle against all attempts by the world to build or maintain walls that divide or separate us from one another or from the love of God. If no one else, the baptized Christian finds the walls of racism's prison intolerable. If nowhere else, in the church should the existing walls be exposed so that together we can tear them down.

Holy Communion has even more power to break through our anesthesia. In the words, "Do this to remember . . . ," we see Holy Communion as a means of creating new consciousness in people suffering from the anesthesia. We are a forgetful people. Our anesthesia encourages us to forget the wall, forget injustice, forget racism. Holy Communion helps to restore our memory. To remember Jesus is to remember everything for which he died; everything for which he gave his life. The most important thing to remember is that we are a community, a restored community, a community that transcends every wall, every barbed wire fence, every national boundary. Holy Communion reminds us of the incredibly exciting and joyful reality that those who live beyond our prison walls are our family. Holy Communion reminds us that our purpose in life is to tear down the walls that divide us.

Institutional Racism in the Church

Each denomination and each congregation of the church functions as an institution. The churches in the United States belong to the long list of institutions whose established functions and activities give society its shape and structure. The unique spiritual function of the church is carried out in a very conventional and familiar structure. Organizationally speaking, it resembles a secular corporation. The church's pastors, priests, deacons, nuns, and other workers are its institutional personnel; its bishops are the chief executive officers. Institutional racism in the church functions much like that of any other organization. It is buried in deliberate, historically traceable decisions of the past and is perpetuated by the intentional and unintentional decisions and actions of the present. As in secular organizations, it exists in layers increasingly difficult to explore and eliminate, beginning with the most accessible layer of personnel, then the more deeply entrenched layers of policy and practice, and finally, most stubborn of all, the deeply embedded racism within the church's structure and foundational base. Each of these categories, already discussed in chapter four, are very much evident in the life of the church.

The institutional identity of the European American church has been largely derived from the models brought to this country by European immigrants. However, the racial exclusiveness of the churches was determined by developments after the immigrants arrived in the United States. One crucial factor in this development was loyalty to the government and allegiance to other white power structures that became part of the church during its early history. At the time of immigration, these churches bore the difficult responsibilities of helping to preserve the culture and lifestyles of the past and helping the new immigrants to adjust and gain acceptance in their adopted land. Thus, the churches often led the way in encouraging assimilation by way of unquestioning loyalty and patriotism. So anxious were they to give their blessing to the state that it became unthinkable to challenge or disagree with popular political beliefs, either on the local or national level. One amazing result of these emerging relationships is the unique tradition in the United States of having a national flag in the sanctuaries of the church. This profound loyalty to the secular powers of early American society does much to explain how the rigid walls of the white racial prison were constructed in the United States.

Decisions by church leaders to develop segregated congregations followed quite naturally from this identification with white secular and political bodies. Likewise, the organization of racially separate church institutions, even separate denominations, becomes more understandable. The decision of several denominations to divide at the time of the Civil War, for example, was simply an extension of political loyalties. These and hundreds of other deliberate, historically traceable decisions have determined not only our status as a segregated church, but also the practices of indirect racism in today's churches. It was, for example, a deliberate and historically traceable decision within some denominations to give their boards of "foreign mission" the assignment to do evangelism among people of color in the United States. It was a deliberate and historically traceable decision in some denominations to develop separate seminaries for people of color. It was, likewise, the result of deliberate and historically traceable decisions after World War II that thousands of congregations from almost every denomination followed their constituencies from the cities to the suburbs because of the influx of people of color. All of these, and many, many other examples demonstrate the deliberate and historically traceable actions of the churches that created the prison in which we find ourselves today.

It must be restated that the purpose of such historical recall is not to condemn the church or create feelings of guilt within people. Rather, our goal is to understand how we become the way we are, so that we can better change the way we will be in the future. As in most institutions, racism in the church today is no longer caused by direct racism and its deliberate decisions. Rather, we are caught in a self-perpetuating system that was created by past decisions and is very difficult to change. Like the rest of society, most white Christians find it difficult to understand that the prison of racism is as secure as ever, even though the intentional racism of the past has been so greatly reduced.

But results are what count, and today our churches are nearly as segregated as they ever were. Furthermore, although the presence of some people of color in the predominantly white churches is a small but encouraging step, it will have minimal impact on institutional racism until it affects the power relationships of corporate decision-making in the churches where they are members. Power is the primary issue in undoing racism. Since it is power in the first place that creates racism out of personal prejudices, power is also primary in resolving racism. As with the New Testament church, at one time it was the power to exclude people of color from entering the church that defined our racism. But now the power to refuse access has been replaced by the power to control those who have been given access. Decisions that affect people of color in our churches are still decided by the white majority. Furthermore, white people continue to be trapped inside a predominantly white church in a predominantly white community, unable to experience the unity we proclaim and seek with the great diversity of God's creation.

Racism in Personnel, Policy, and Structure

Now let us look briefly at some examples of the church's institutional racism in each of the three organizational levels: personnel; policy and practice; structures and foundations.

Personnel. In the case of the church, personnel refers first of all to its professional staff—priests, pastors, deacons, deaconesses, religious orders, theologians, educators, administrators, musicians, custodians, and other paid church workers. Also included, however, are volunteer leaders, committee and board members, teachers, and other elected and appointed workers. Through their perceptions, attitudes, and behavior, all of these people provide for others the primary impressions, either of a church that is racist or a church with a commitment to work for an end to racism. A single person can give the entire church a positive or negative institutional image. A pastor, Sunday school teacher, or committee member can project to others the image of either a racist church or a church that is struggling to overcome its racism and build a new multiracial identity.

Today many seminaries offer a variety of courses to prepare clergy for more effective work in multiracial and cross-cultural situations. These opportunities for education and direct experience need to be more intense, and they also need to resolve a significant contradiction. Seldom is there comparable input into the training of clergy for suburban or predominantly white situations, where there is a far greater need for confronting racism and building a multicultural consciousness.

Policy and Practice. Like every corporate entity, the church creates institutional policy and then seeks to implement that policy in its practices. We need to remember, however, that there is no such thing as a nonracist in a racist society. A person or an institution acts in a way that will either promote or combat racism. As long as there is racism to contend with, a policy or practice of the church will be either racist or antiracist in its intent and effect.

An institution's racism in policy and practice can be seen, for example, in its policies for ordained personnel, since they determine the recruitment, selection, training, endorsement, assignment, evaluation, and discipline of clergy. These policies affect the number of persons of color on the church's clergy roster, the assignment of clergy of color to white congregations, the relationship between white clergy and clergy of color, and the responsibility to teach about and work to eliminate racism among their white parishioners.

The domestic mission policies of the church are often hampered by racism. These policies determine, among other things, how many new mission congregations will be organized in white communities and in communities of other racial and ethnic backgrounds. Even more importantly, these policies determine how mission work in poor urban communities is supported, evaluated, and continued. In recent years most denominations have, in fact, improved their policies in these areas and have made commitments to develop a greater number of mission churches in communities of color. It will be important to monitor over the next few years the degree to which this policy is being implemented. The current economic pressure on most denominations, unfortunately, poses a great danger that commitments already made to work in areas with no immediate financial returns will be cut back.

Of crucial importance are the policies of the church that concern social issues. Such policies give the church its public image and determine how it will work for justice in the larger society. As for policies concerning issues of racism and racial justice, both the church's official position and how that position is developed are important. Even if the church's stand with regard to an issue of racial justice is seen as progressive, that position will be perceived as patronizing and racist if the persons of color who are affected by the issue do not take primary leadership in the deliberations and decision-making.

Structures and Foundations. As with any other institution, racism at the level of the church's structures and foundational base is very difficult to identify and eliminate. A vivid illustration of structural racism may be seen in the distribution of power in the church's decision-making. In local congregations as well as in the structures of national denominations, one often finds that although persons of color may be present in significant numbers, they lack proportionate representation in positions of power, and they lack the votes. A related problem manifests itself when white congregations find themselves in racial transition. Often when the membership of people of color approaches the point of becoming a majority, a significant exodus of the remaining white members occurs. Another variation on this theme: Often when only a few white people remain as members, they are still the primary decision-makers. A final example: Some churches in racially changing communities encourage a second congregation under the same roof. This often happens when the second congregation speaks another language, usually Spanish or an Asian language. Such an arrangement can lead to several difficulties. First, the new congregation feels patronized and controlled by the resident white congregation. Second, further problems may develop when the new congregation begins to rival in size the white congregation that helped to develop the mission, either because the mission is growing or the white membership is dwindling. The white congregation often has great difficulty in facing the loss of its ability to be the primary decision-maker.

Another kind of structural racism that is devastating but rarely acknowledged or analyzed can be seen when denominational administration for urban and surburban mission is separated. Although policy and practice will understandably in many ways be different for these two quite different situations, one also finds a contradictory understanding of mission emerging because of the separation between these two units. Emphasis on social justice, for example, is considered to be a central focus of urban ministry. There is even the frequent expectation that this emphasis will be defined in fairly radical ways. But there are few comparable expectations in the middle- and upper-class surburbs. Social concerns, if dealt with at all, are compartmentalized in a social ministry committee and have little effect on the total ministry of the congregation.

Finally, we need to address racism in the church's foundations: in the underlying purpose, the spiritual and moral teaching, and the historical tradition. At first glance, it may seem surprising that the church could suffer from such deeply rooted racism. What could be more holy than the moral and spiritual teaching of love, peace, and forgiveness? What could be less subject to question than the church's underlying purpose of bringing God's justice and reconciliation to the world? Certainly there can be no fundamental racism in the underlying purposes or in the moral and spiritual teachings. On the other hand, we have identified a number of problems in the church's historical tradition that can hardly be explained away as problems of personnel, policy, or even structure. What role, for example, does racism play in the continuing tension between the church's schizophrenic personalities: the triumphal and servant churches? Or how does one account for the irresistibly fatal attraction between church and empire—an attraction that leads inevitably to the coopting of the church and the betrayal of its mission? And, even more directly, how do we explain the anti-Semitism in key documents of the Reformation that has plagued the church for centuries? And, is it not somewhere in those foundations of the church that we must face and find the reason for the shameful segregation that still divides American Christianity into separate racial denominations?

To combat racism will require extended effort. It will demand of us careful and dedicated work on the levels of personnel, policy, and structure. At the same time, careful and courageous exploration must continue to determine how much of the racism that imprisons the church will not be rooted out until we rebuild the church's very foundations.

Cultural Racism in the Church

Culture plays a principal role in communicating and transmitting religious form and content. Likewise, religion has an important role in creating and transforming culture. The extent and the limits of this mutual interaction are the subject of much theological debate, but there is no denying the fundamental importance of the relationship. Increasing emphasis is being placed on the central role of culture in building a racially inclusive, pluralistic church and society. Before we can address the positive task of building a multicultural church, however, we must be aware of the ways in which we have used culture as a tool of racism. Cultural racism has deeply affected the church in the United States in at least three ways.

First, the cultural gifts of other racial and ethnic groups have been excluded from the church. In the context of the five dominant racial/cultural groupings in the United States, the European American church has remained a monocultural church. (This, of course, does not address the many European subcultures it represents. Each of the major racial/cultural groupings in the United States—African American, Native American, Asian, Hispanic, and European American—is comprised of many separate national and ethnic cultures. However, seen as one of five major racial/cultural groupings, the European American church, sadly, is still a monocultural church.)

The European American church participated with the rest of white society in creating the cultural curtain that has separated white culture from other racial and ethnic cultures in our society. It has also joined in preventing the "cultural conflict" necessary to develop a truly American multicultural society. The cultures and the traditions of African Americans, Asians, Hispanics, and Native Americans have been excluded and marginalized within the churches in the United States just as they have been excluded and marginalized in secular society. It is important, however, to add a note of celebration. The religious traditions and cultures of people of color have not only survived, but they have flourished and continue to be crucial in the struggle to survive the effects of racist exploitation.

Cultural racism is expressed in many other ways in the European American churches. In worship forms, education, and other aspects of religious lifestyle, God and Jesus are overwhelmingly portrayed with European features. The church's music and art, as well as its moral and ethical values, are derived almost exclusively from Europe. The variety of cultures of people of color are made to seem inferior when, for example, the teachings of the faith are communicated to them entirely in the cultural symbols and language of the European American society. European theological language and categories, in particular, are valued more highly than those from elsewhere. This is abundantly clear from the churches' response to liberation theology and other theological contributions of the third world. In another aspect of cultural racism, linguistic racism becomes magnified a hundred-fold when words such as "white," "bright," and "light" are used to speak of God, purity, sinlessness, and forgiveness, and when we use words such as "black" and "dark" to speak of sin, evil, death, and the devil.

Second, cultural racism has been harmful to the white church as well. The effects of isolation have been disastrous, and while confrontation with other expressions within the church could provide the basis for the development of new and stronger cultural forms, the absence of such confrontation has been severely limited. We do not deny the strength and beauty of the European church's cultural expressions. However, in their continued isolation, most of these churches still reflect exclusively their European background, with little that is new and creative. When they participated in locking other racial and ethnic cultures out of the white community, the white churches also helped to lock themselves into a situation that can only bring spiritual weakness, stagnation, and death if allowed to go unchallenged and unchanged.

Third, the European American church still expects assimilation and acculturalization by people of color when they join the church. Certainly these denominations take a positive step by placing a high priority on inclusiveness. However, the issue is how much a church is willing to change in order to accommodate these new members. Unfortunately, one of the greatest temptations is to not want to make any change; rather, if there is changing to be done, let it be an entry requirement for the new members of color. This, in fact, is what many people of color are experiencing when they join a European American denomination. Not surprisingly, it is one of the major objections by people of color to the white churches' denominational evangelism and membership recruitment programs. As we said, the modern equivalent to the "circumcision crowd" of the New Testament are white members who insist that people of color must become cultural Europeans before they can become members. Acculturalization becomes a requirement for church membership. If people of color think theologically like European Americans, sing and worship like European Americans, and fit into an organizational design and structure that is European American, they may become true members of the church.

The issue becomes even more complex, however, for it is not simply a question of what cultural expression the church will have for people of races and ethnic backgrounds other than ours. The question is also the kind of continuing cultural expression the church will have for European Americans. This question becomes the most obvious in congregations with a significant number of members of more than one cultural tradition. In such a setting, the calling is clear to create a means by which mutual sharing and learning can take place so that everyone can begin to celebrate the faith in their own cultural language and symbols, and also learn the language and symbols of another culture.

But what about the majority of congregations in the European American community that are still predominantly or totally white? Should they not also be learning to experience and express the faith multiculturally? It does not seem appropriate that they wait until their congregation becomes multicultural in membership before they discover and experience the multicultural nature of the church. For the issue is not just that of accommodating people of other races and cultures, but rather the need for all of us to experience and to learn to celebrate the faith in other than European American symbols. Only in this way will we all participate in the task of transforming the European American church into a multicultural American church.

If the New Testament church had not resolved its difficulties, but had instead created two churches, one for Jews and one for Gentiles, the church would never have gotten beyond scandalous parochial expression to discover its truly universal nature. If Christianity in the United States does not resolve its problems as did the New Testament church, it will continue to be bound by the scandal of racial segregation, with a different church for either side of the ghetto walls—a living contradiction of God's gifts of unity and the reconciliation that we celebrate each Sunday morning. C. Eric Lincoln speaks a loud "Amen!" to this, and calls us to become what God intends us to be:

> The White Church needs to consider the range of its opportunities and responsibilities. The legal color line is dead. Forever. It was a painful and unfortunate experiment in the human attempt to be more than human at the expense of being humane. It failed because there is only one order of humanity, and whatever the range of human aptitude and capability, it is neither more nor less than what it is. Human. The White Church needs the means to deal with this far more effectively than it has in the context of its ministry. The legal color line is dead, but once again that is our dilemma. We are still captives of a psychological color line, and our principal sensitivities and commitments remain coded to a schedule of values which magnify our differences rather than celebrate what we have in common. . . .
>
> Our dilemma is that the energies we ought to reserve to contain the ever-increasing threats to our survival as a nation and as a civilization continue dissipated over issues that are no longer viable, and the continuing harvest is inevitable bitterness, discord and futility. The resolution of our dilemma is in the critical interest of God and country. And it may be that, in the resolute pursuit of a common task of such challenge and magnitude, black religion and white religion will someday rediscover the larger community of interests they knew when the church was neither white nor black but just simply a fellowship of believers.[9]

7

FROM RACISM TO PLURALISM

---

*There is a time for everything, and a season
for every activity under heaven . . . a time to
tear down and a time to build. . . .*
—*Ecclesiastes 3:1, 3 NIV*

In the preceding chapters we have tried to say in many ways that
a multiracial and multicultural society cannot be built unless we
are willing to look at, learn about, confront, and work to dismantle white racism. The goal of this final chapter is to point out directions that take us beyond dismantling racism to the building of
a racially just and pluralistic society.

A Time to Tear Down

To study racism is to study walls. We have looked at barriers and
fences, restraints and limitations, ghettos and prisons. The prison
of racism confines us all, people of color and white people alike.
It shackles the victimizer as well as the victim. The walls forcibly
keep people of color and white people separate from each other;
in our separate prisons we are all prevented from achieving the
human potential that God intends for us. The limitations imposed on people of color by poverty, subservience, and powerlessness are cruel, inhuman, and unjust; the effects of uncon-

trolled power, privilege, and greed, which are the marks of our white prison, will inevitably destroy us as well. But we have also seen that the walls of racism can be dismantled. We are not condemned to an inexorable fate, but are offered the vision and the possibility of freedom. Brick by brick, stone by stone, the prison of individual, institutional, and cultural racism can be destroyed. You and I are urgently called to join the efforts of those who know it is time to tear down, once and for all, the walls of racism.

The danger point of self-destruction seems to be drawing ever more near. The results of centuries of national and worldwide conquest and colonialism, of military buildups and violent aggression, of overconsumption and environmental destruction may be reaching a point of no return. A small and predominantly white minority of the global population derives its power and privilege from the sufferings of the vast majority of peoples of color. For the sake of the world and ourselves, we dare not allow it to continue.

An Invitation to Conspiracy

Walls do not fall of their own accord. Injustice comes to an end when there are strong enough forces to oppose it. Each of us is called to join an evergrowing global coalition to dismantle racism and other forms of exploitation.

There is a profound belief among oppressed people that they are destined to be free, a faith that their suffering will come to an end. We have seen evidence all around us in recent years that this belief is well founded. Walls have indeed been crumbling in Germany and Russia, South Africa, Namibia, and elsewhere. But these walls are not collapsing from their own weight while people sit back and wait for their freedom. They are falling because people refuse to accept the terms of their imprisonment. Oppressed peoples of eastern Europe and southern Africa, in the United States and throughout the world are participants in shaping the coalition of forces that cause these walls to crash down.

"Conspiracy" is an even more accurate word to describe these united efforts. There is, indeed, a global conspiracy to tear down the walls of oppression all over the world. In a sense, the FBI and the CIA have been right all along. An international subversive plot is afoot, aimed not only at the United States but also at the entire white western world. This conspiracy is terrifying to those who support and benefit from the sufferings of others. But it is good news to those who wait for justice and release.

Where the FBI and the CIA have been wrong, however, is in the identity of the conspirators. For years they have been arming themselves against the wrong enemy. Until recently, at least, they believed they were fighting a communist conspiracy, and they had names like "tools of the communists" for persons who participated in its activities. Now, communism is no longer a threat. Yet, to the dismay of these global detectives, the conspiracy continues unabated. Eventually, those who opposed communism will have to draw the conclusion that many have been pointing out to them for years: the conspiracy does indeed exist, but the conspirators are not who they thought they were.

Who, then, are the real leaders of this conspiracy? This is, in fact, a coalition of three major powers. The first of these conspirators is a great mass of people from the two thirds of the world that is poor and oppressed. It does indeed include communists, but also a great many other people representing a wide variety of political ideologies, national philosophies, racial and ethnic identities, and religious faiths. From the United States, it includes people of color, as well as a significant number of whites who are rejecting the privilege and power of their nationality and race. At times, this mass of people seems weak and divided, a rag-tag army of protest that is repeatedly defeated and destroyed. At other times, one can see and feel in it the power of a liberation army, sure and certain of its victory over oppression.

The second of the three conspirators is the whole creation. The heavens and the earth, in open rebellion against neglect and destruction, against poisons and pollution, against rape and ravage, are no longer willing to use their recuperative powers to perpetuate evil. They are permitting us to be sickened by the fouling of our own nest. As the earth runs out of resources, it refuses to produce more for a technology based on greed, and designed for excess consumption and waste. From the bowels of the earth comes the cry, "Enough!" Nature herself has joined the conspiracy against those who would subject the world to their selfish goals.

The third of the conspirators is by far the most powerful of the three. It is the Creator of the universe, the designer of history, the God of Abraham, Isaac, and Jacob, of Rachel, Ruth, and Rebecca, whose passion for a whole and just universe is as strong as ever, and whose anger toward those who divide and oppress God's people, who exploit and destroy the creation is as fearful as ever. The same God who once spoke through the prophets of old speaks as clearly to us now:

> I hate, I despise your festivals, and I take no delight in your solemn assemblies. Even though you offer me your burnt offerings and grain offerings, I will not accept them; and the offerings of well-being of your fatted animals I will not look upon. Take away from me the noise of your songs; I will not listen to the melody of your harps. But let justice roll down like waters, and righteousness like an everflowing stream. (Amos 5:21-24)

Our first response to the reality of this conspiracy is likely to be apprehension and fear. As has already been pointed out, our loyalties have been aligned with those who maintain the prison walls, and we derive a great many benefits from them. The world as we know it will go through drastic changes as racism is dismantled and other forms of exploitation are ended. The end goal of the conspiracy, however, is freedom for all—of every race and nation. Whatever our position in life, we stand to gain infinitely more than we can lose from this conspiracy of the Creator, the creation, and the great majority of the world's people.

You and I are also invited to join this conspiracy. We are called, wherever we live, work, or play to join the task of tearing down the walls, brick by brick. However, the invitation is an urgent one. "We shall have to hurry," writes C. Eric Lincoln, "for history is as cynical as it is inexorable. The wheel must turn, and is turning."[1]

In a presentation to a convocation of the World Council of Churches, Jim Wallis, editor of *Sojourners*, spoke to the urgency of the task:

History will overtake the west as well. It's only a matter of time. Here, too, the system is failing while we struggle to keep up the illusions. Our inner cities, which have become war zones, are but the first sign of a global economy that is unravelling.

The historic events we witness today are prophetic. Today it is the east wind of freedom and democracy that is blowing out the old. Tomorrow it will be a south wind of justice and liberation to set free the oppressed. . . . When the south wind blows with the hopes of the world's poor on its wings, it will cause a chilly gale to be felt by those northern global power centres that now run the world's system of economic apartheid.

Today an ugly wall of ideological repression is crumbling down. Tomorrow the invisible walls of international trade, finance and economic oppression will also come tumbling down. It's hard to stop the wind when it begins to blow.[2]

And a Time to Build

We will need many more reminders that we cannot build a pluralistic society without tearing down the walls of racism. However, this same reminder must be turned around and stated inversely; we cannot tear down the walls without the intention and commitment to build new communities that are inclusive and pluralistic. Jesus said that when a demon is cast out, we must take care not to leave its place or residence unoccupied, lest it return with seven other evil spirits more wicked than before and reoccupy the house. We must go from racism to pluralism. The bricks that were used to build the walls of the prison must now be used for a better purpose. Just as we tear down, brick by brick, so also must we build new structures of justice.

Creating multicultural institutions is as important as eliminating institutional racism. During the past few years a rapidly increasing supply of information and resources has become available to assist in this task.[3] Many schools, churches, corporations, and governmental institutions are on this new frontier, seeking to discover and define more accurately the nature of a pluralistic society. According to one definition, a multi-cultural organization:

- reflects the contributions and interests of diverse cultural and social groups in its mission, operations, and product or service;

- acts on a commitment to eradicate social oppression in all forms within the organization;

- includes the members of diverse cultural and social groups as full participants, especially in decisions that shape the organization; and

- follows through on broader external social responsibilities, including support of efforts to eliminate all forms of social oppression and to educate others in multicultural perspectives.[4]

Those who read this book are encouraged to prepare themselves to take the next step beyond dismantling racism. Moving from monocultural to multicultural institutions and life-styles is a difficult and complex task. It is also exciting and rewarding. Is there not within each of us a deep longing for the community that was lost or never realized? This longing becomes even more intense as we begin to remove the barriers that have prevented such a sense of community from being fulfilled. Is it not exciting to contemplate new freedom and diversity in our own lives, in our circles of friends, in the organizations through which we participate in struggles for justice, in the churches where we worship, in the other institutions and communities of our daily life, and even in more distant national and global structures? Is it not liberating to realize our potential for creating multiracial and multicultural communities in which gifts are willingly shared and received, in which openness and trust can take the place of fear and hostility, in which we can work together and struggle together to build new structures that are just and egalitarian? Is it not a source of deepest joy to believe that we can yet fulfill the intentions of God's creation?

The Role of White People

The invitation to participate in building a pluralistic society has special meaning for white people and requires our willingness to ask some straightforward questions about ourselves. Many of us once used an old racist phrase to describe the confidence we have in our power. When someone said we couldn't do something, we would answer, "Why not? I'm free, white, and twenty-one!" Being white, in the previously quoted words of Robert Terry, means not having to think about it. Now that we *do* want to think about it, perhaps the most important question for us is, What does it mean to be white? And, now that we know we are not free, what does it mean to become free and white? These questions are addressed to us both as individuals and as part of the larger white community. We can no longer take the answers to these questions for granted. We can no longer seek relationships with people of color while maintaining our privilege and power.

In an interracial workshop setting, one of the most revealing experiences is to hear how members of different racial groups answer the question, "What do I like most about being white, black, red, yellow, or brown?" For people of color the answers almost always relate to cultural characteristics and strengths that have evolved out of their struggle to survive in an unjust world. For white people the answers almost always relate to benefits derived from having privilege and power. When white people are then asked a second question, "What do you like about being white apart from things requiring special privilege and power?", they find the question very difficult to answer.

We need to ask ourselves two other questions: "What have we lost as white people because of racism?" and "What have we to gain with the end of racism?" These questions become easier to answer as we become more aware of the extent to which racism imprisons us. For we have lost so very much, and we have so very much to gain. As each of us struggles with these questions, we need to look for answers that are clear and that speak to the urgent necessity for change in our lives. If we are to have a lasting commitment to the struggle, we need also to know how we ourselves will benefit from a world without racism.

A New White People

These questions raise still further questions about our identity. At issue is not only our identity as individuals, but our collective identity as a white people. Many of us who have a European heritage are deeply attached to our cultural past, given us by our fore-parents. Our immediate need, however, is to struggle with our present racial and cultural identity. It is this identity of ourselves as European Americans that will be our contribution at the multicultural table as we seek to develop a truly multiracial and multicultural American identity.

This search for our identity will require of us a better understanding of United States history and the role our people have played in it. In part, this is important so that we may understand the things of which we must repent and the things we must change. It is also important because we need to learn about the exciting and good part of our history. It is a part of our history that most of us have never learned and that will help us to develop a vision of what we can become. Who, for example, are the white people in our history who resisted the forces of racism, who fought for abolition, who tried to stop the genocide of Native Americans, who gave their lives in the struggle for justice? In our religious and cultural celebrations, we can disassociate ourselves from the national heroes and heroines that have been foisted on us uncritically and about whom we feel little but shame for their violence and destruction. We can instead discover, lift up, and celebrate new heroes and heroines with whom we can identify, for whom we can feel pride, and who we want to imitate. Above all, we need to develop an identity and a unity with our own people that is not based on privilege and power. We need to develop a passion and love for them that seeks their freedom from the prison of racism. There is much that we can learn from people of color. Their oppression has caused them to rediscover continually the strength of unity and mutual caring that is the basis of survival and freedom. Can we develop this same love for white people and for ourselves as a community? Can we develop the same passion for one another's freedom?

From Monoculture to Multiculture

As white people who participate in multiracial coalitions and organizations, we must learn two hard lessons. One is the ability to follow the leadership of people of color. This is very hard for us, since it is at the very core of racism that whites should lead and people of color follow. Second, if we no longer lead, it is hard to avoid the opposite temptation: to stand on the sidelines and limit our participation to mere cheering. We are not just supporters of people of color, but co-participants in this struggle for the freedom of us all. Eliminating racism is an equal opportunity task that welcomes all participants.

Building pluralistic communities requires broad vision as well as specific commitment. This vision, if it is to work, will be shaped by asking some very pragmatic questions. What kinds of social structures meet the needs of all people and cultures? How do nonracist institutions function? What are the alternatives to the present economic system? What viable methods and strategies exist for feeding, housing, and clothing everyone in a given neighborhood, city, country? How do we create a workable multicultural existence? Who should control and distribute resources? Such questions cannot be answered, even within the context of small institutions and communities, by people whose orientation and experience do not extend beyond the white western world. Neither the needs of other people nor even our own needs can be evaluated and dealt with in terms of a monocultural orientation and value system. Intentionally or not, it would inevitably result in continued exploitation and manipulation.

Finally, creating a pluralistic society is a hands-on task; it does not come about through words that express our good intentions but rather through specific definable efforts and actions. The creating of multiracial institutions and communities requires that all who live and work in them help to develop goals and strategies, education and training, implementation and evaluation. It requires a personal commitment to openness, honesty, willingness to take risks, and to participate fully. Moreover, it cannot be done either from the top down, authoritatively, or from the bottom up, anarchistically. It calls for dual commitments from top to bottom and from bottom to top. The organization's leaders and every member of the organization or community must be fully recognized participants in the process.

Above all, the commitment must be a long-term effort. This kind of in-depth organizational and community change does not happen quickly. It encompasses many stages of growth and transformation with more than a few setbacks and re-starts along the way. But at the same time, each step of the way, participants should expect to experience increasingly the freedom from imprisonment that we have described in earlier chapters.

Now Is the Time: A "Kairos Moment"

Only time will tell if racism can be overcome. Only time will tell if a process of conversion and change will be set in motion through the "conspiracy" we have described. Only time will tell if we can create a truly multiracial and multicultural society. But there is no question what time it is now, and what we are called upon to be and do. For the very time in which we live is the moment of truth. In the words of Martin Luther King Jr.:

> We are faced with the fierce urgency of now. . . . This may well be [hu]mankind's last chance to choose between chaos or community.[5]

At this very moment, the United States faces an escalating crisis in race relations. Today that crisis is more severe than yesterday. Tomorrow, it is fair to assume, the situation will be more urgent than today. In response to this crisis, our old friend the servant church has once again become more visible. A growing number of Christians, not only in the United States but throughout the world, are reacting with great emotion to the tragic suffering of so many people and to the use of the Christian faith to support the very governmental policies that bring about this suffering. They are angered and shocked by the failure of the churches to speak out in protest against such actions by the United States and other governments throughout the world.

In recent years Christians in southern Africa, Central America, and Asia have joined together to interpret the time in which we live as a "kairos moment" in history. *Kairos,* an ancient Greek word, means "a crisis or opportunity." It is a special moment in time. A kairos moment is usually unplanned and unexpected, is filled with anticipation, and contains both crisis and opportunity. These third-world Christians have published a number of "kairos documents" addressing the seriousness of the crisis that confronts the church and the world.[6] The following excerpts are from a well-known recent South African Kairos Document:

> The time has come. The moment of truth has arrived. South Africa has been plunged into a crisis that is shaking the foundations. . . . It is the Kairos, or moment of truth not only for apartheid but also for the church. This is the Kairos, the moment of grace and opportunity, the favorable time in which God issues a challenge to decisive action. It is a dangerous time because if this opportunity is missed and allowed to pass by, the loss for the church, for the Gospel, and for all the people of South Africa will be immeasurable. . . . We are convinced that this challenge comes from God, and that it is addressed to all of us. We see the present crisis or Kairos as indeed a divine visitation.[7]

We in the United States are also living on the edge of a kairos moment of truth, which thrusts itself on us in the form of a crisis and offers itself to us as an opportunity. For those of us who are trapped in racism's despair and powerlessness, it is a moment of empowerment, a time for the banner of justice to be lifted once again, and of the demands for human rights to be heard once more. For those who live in comfort and security, who have fallen into complacency, it is time to be awakened from their sleep and be troubled by the pressing realities of racism and poverty. For Christians in the United States, this is a kairos moment.

The Year 2000 A.D.

Perhaps the single most vivid symbol of this kairos moment is the rapidly approaching turn of the millennium—a promise of new beginnings. The final decade of the old millennium should be a time of anticipation and planning for that opportunity. As the time draws closer, there will be a sense of urgency and resolve the world over to enter the new century with a commitment to achieve national and world unity and community and to live in justice and peace. It is an opportunity for us as a nation to leave behind our tragic heritage of racism and enter a new millennium of racial and ethnic pluralism.

According to current projections, we will not be long into the twenty-first century before 51 percent of the population in the United States will be people of color. It is truly an approaching kairos moment, a time when we are given the opportunity to re-think what it means to be American and to restructure our country in ways that reflect who we really are.

The closing words of the Road to Damascus document on kairos and confession shall conclude this book as well. For both end on the same note of a kairos moment, a moment that calls the church to conversion and new hope:

All of us who profess to be followers of Jesus of Nazareth are in continuous need of conversion. While we see clearly the idolatry, the heresy, the hypocrisy and the blasphemy of others, we ourselves need to search our own hearts for remnants of the same sins and for signs of triumphalism, self-righteousness, dogmatism, rigidity, intolerance and sectarianism. There should be no place in our hearts for any kind of complacency.

This proclamation was written and signed to give an account of the hope that is in us. Like the disciples who travelled along the road to Emmaus we are sometimes tempted to give up hope. As the two disciples say: "Our own hope had been that he (Jesus) would be the one to set Israel free" (Luke 24:21). What they still had to learn from Jesus and what we need to be reminded of again and again is that the way to freedom and salvation is the way of the cross. "Was it not ordained that Christ should suffer and so enter into his glory?" (Luke 24:26). There is no cheap salvation or liberation. There is no easy road.

Because of our faith in Jesus, we are bold enough to hope for something that fulfills and transcends all human expectations, namely the Reign of God. We are even called to live with the hope that those who collaborate with the idols of death and those who persecute us today will be converted to the God of life.[8]

Within our churches and together with Christians from every part of the world, we must seize this opportunity to face once again the struggle between the servant church and the triumphal church. Our efforts to overcome racism must begin in our own sanctuaries and continue beyond the church to create a nation and a world in which all races and cultures are included, accepted, and enabled to live together in equality and harmony.

NOTES

Introduction

1. Regarding the use of "people of color": there is constant change in the commonly accepted terms describing various racial and ethnic groups in U.S. society. Oftentimes the reason for the changes are that terms become misused and take on offensive or racist significance. At the time of this writing, "people of color" has replaced the term "minority groups," and the most common terms for the five major U.S. racial/ethnic groupings are African American, Native American, Hispanic, Asian, and European American (or simply, white). It is not unlikely that these or other current terms used in this book will be replaced. It is hoped that the meanings will nevertheless be understood. However, should any of these terms take on an offensive meaning, the author apologizes in advance.

2. Regarding the phrase "mission to white people": as of this writing, the end of the South African system of apartheid seems to be on the horizon, although it will clearly not come about without a great deal more struggle. One of the most serious questions that is now beginning to be raised in South Africa is how to do antiracism education among white people of that country. Thus, the task, "mission to white people" is being explored by the South African Council of Churches, the Institute for Contextual Theology, Koinonia, and a number of other more forward thinking and acting groups. Although there is a great deal that is different in the South African situation, there is also much that is quite similar to our situation in the United States. In the task of dismantling racism, the two countries have a lot to learn from each other.

3. Martin Luther King Jr., "Where Do We Go from Here: Chaos or Community?" cited from *A Testament of Hope: The Essential Writings of Martin Lu-*

ther King, Jr., edited by James M. Washington (San Francisco: Harper and Row, 1986), 623.

Chapter 1

1. Martin Luther King Jr., "Facing the Challenge of a New Age," an address before the First Annual Institute on Non-Violence and Social Change, held in Montgomery, Alabama, December 1956; recorded in *A Testament of Hope: The Essential Writings of Martin Luther King, Jr.*, edited by James M. Washington (San Francisco: Harper and Row, 1986), 141.

2. If they have not already done so, readers are encouraged to develop a thorough knowledge and understanding of the civil rights movement as well as other aspects of a more comprehensive and complete U.S. history. See the bibliography for resources, among which is the very helpful film/video series, "Eyes on the Prize."

3. C. Eric Lincoln, *Race, Religion and the Continuing American Dilemma* (New York: Hill and Wang, 1984), 10, 11.

4. From a news conference reported by the *New York Times*, July 10, 1989, 7.

5. The studies and polls taken throughout the United States at the end of the 1980s and the beginning of the 1990s include the following:

    A Common Destiny: Blacks and American Society, edited by Gerald David Jaynes and Robin M. Williams Jr. (Washington D.C.: National Academy Press, 1989). This is a landmark 588-page study by the National Research Council, described by *Time* as the "most definitive report card on race relations in 20 years. And America has flunked."

    A Lou Harris poll, conducted for the NAACP Legal Defensive Fund, released in 1989 and available from the NAACP offices, P.O. Box 13064, New York, NY 10277.

    A poll by the newspaper *USA Today* in September 1989.

    All of these polls take great pains to study objectively the current situation in the United States and to identify where progress has been made. In each case, the report concludes that, despite significant progress in some areas, racism is as bad or worse than ever and the results of racism as devastating as ever.

6. Sources: Center on Budget and Policy Priorities, and The Defense Budget Project, Washington, D.C., 1991.

7. Lou Harris poll, NAACP, 1989.

8. From a study released by The Sentencing Project, Washington, D.C., in February 1990. The study was based on an analysis of 1989 statistics of the U.S. Bureau of Justice.

9. See William Julius Wilson, *The Truly Disadvantaged: The Inner City, the Underclass, and Public Policy* (Chicago: University of Chicago Press, 1987).

10. Kenneth Lipper, ex-Deputy Mayor of New York City, "What Needs to Be Done?," *New York Times Magazine*, December 31, 1989, p. 28.

11. The term "third world" is used here and elsewhere in this book to refer to the poor nations of Africa, Asia, and Central and South America. It is also used occasionally as an alternative term for poor people of color in the United States. This term is not universally accepted. Some prefer the term "two-thirds world," referring to the portion of population represented rather than to their third-class status. Third world is the term used here, since it is currently the most widely used and accepted.

12. Tyrone Pitts, "Racism and the U.S. Economy," *PCR Information*, a publication of the World Council of Churches' Programme to Combat Racism, 1987/No. 24, 28.

Chapter 2

1. The "Big Foot Analysis" was developed by the People's Institute for Survival and Beyond, a national network of antiracism trainers and organizers based at 1444 North Johnson Street, New Orleans, LA 70116.

2. Lincoln, *Race, Religion and the Continuing American Dilemma*, 8-11.

3. See the *Report of the National Advisory Commission on Civil Disorders* known as the Kerner Report (New York: Bantam Books, 1968).

4. Will Campbell, *Brother to a Dragonfly* (New York: Continuum, 1988), 222.

5. Jim Wallis, *America's Original Sin: A Study Guide on White Racism* (Washington, D.C.: Sojourners Resource Center, 1988), 9.

6. Lincoln, *Race, Religion and the Continuing American Dilemma*, 3.

7. From notes on a lecture by Dr. Albert Pero, professor of systematic theology at Lutheran School of Theology at Chicago, presented at Holden Village, Chelan, Washington, August 1989.

Chapter 3

1. C. S. Lewis, *The Great Divorce* (New York: Macmillan, 1946), 18ff.

2. An important study of internalized anger is Price Cobbs and William Grier's *Black Rage* (New York: Basic Books, 1980). Also see Catherine Meeks, "Rage and Reconciliation: Two Sides of the Same Coin," *America's Original Sin: A Study Guide on White Racism*, 98ff.

3. Robert Terry, "The Negative Impact on White Values," *Impacts of Racism on White Americans*, edited by Benjamin P. Bowser and Raymond Hunt (Newbury Park, Calif.: Sage Publications, 1981), 120.

4. Ibid., 150.

5. "A Class Divided," a PBS video produced by Public Broadcasting Service, 1320 Braddock Place, Alexandria, VA 22314.

6. Michael Omi and Howard Winant, *Racial Formation in the United States from the 1960s to the 1980s* (New York: Routledge and Kegan Paul, 1986), 63.

7. Terry, "The Negative Impact on White Values," 120.

8. Meeks, "Rage and Reconciliation: Two Sides of the Same Coin," 99.

9. Daniel Goleman, "Psychologists Find Ways to Break Racism's Hold," *New York Times*, September 5, 1989, C1.

10. Ed Kinane, "My Name Is Ed. I'm a Racist," *Fellowship*, July/August 1988, 21.

Chapter 4

1. Omi and Winant, *Racial Formation in the United States from the 1960s to the 1980s*, 115–116.

2. "White Supremacy and Hate Violence: A Decade Review 1980–1990," from Klanwatch Project, 400 Washington Ave., Montgomery, AL 36195.

3. *Dollars and Sense*, April 1990, 23.

4. Wallis, *America's Original Sin: A Study Guide on White Racism*, 9.

Chapter 5

1. *Webster's New Collegiate Dictionary* (Springfield: G. & C. Merriam, 1979), 274.

2. William McClain, *Travelling Light* (New York: Friendship, 1981), 56, 57.

3. Israel Zangwill, *The Melting Pot: Drama in Four Acts* (New York: Macmillan, 1921), 35 ff.

4. *Sojourners*, September/October 1990, 1.

5. John Hightower, "Who Are the Culturally Deprived?," *Saturday Review*, 1970.

6. McClain, *Travelling Light*, 81.

7. Ibid., 92.

8. From a document from an international consultation on the churches' response to racism in the 1980s, quoted by Rob Van Drimmelen in "Racism and Economics—An Ecumenical Concern," *The Economic Basis of Racism* (Geneva: World Council of Churches, 1987), 10.

9. Ralph Winter, *The Twenty-Five Unbelievable Years* (South Pasadena: William Casey Library, 1970).

10. *Low Intensity Warfare: Counterinsurgency, Proinsurgency, and Antiterrorism in the Eighties*, edited by Michael T. Klare and Peter Kornbluh (New York: Pantheon, 1988), 48.

11. Jack Nelson-Pallmeyer, *War Against the Poor: Low Intensity Conflict and Christian Faith* (Maryknoll, N.Y.: Orbis, 1989), xi, 5.

Chapter 6

1. Genesis 9:18-27. This distortion of the Bible has a fascinating history. It has been popularly believed for centuries in virtually every part of the world, and has been promulgated particularly by right-wing hate groups such as the Ku Klux Klan.

Professor Gunther Wittenberg, from the University of Natal in South Africa, has done an interesting new and careful exegetical study and interpretation of this biblical story. He concludes that the descendants of Shem and Ham do not represent Africans or any other ethnic group or race of people, but rather represent social and political systems. He further concludes that "in the present South African system, the true children of Ham are not the blacks

... [but] the whites who have attempted to erect a new Tower of Babel in their 'system' of exploitation and oppression." Similarly, one would conclude that those who have inherited the "curse," or the judgment of God, in the United States are not those who are oppressed by racism but rather those who maintain the racist system. Address requests for this study to Professor G. Wittenburg, Department of Theological Studies, University of Natal, Pietermaritzberg, South Africa.

2. The primary biblical sources for this discussion are Acts 10–15, as well as the central themes of St. Paul's letters to the Romans, the Corinthians, and the Galatians.

3. For a thorough exploration of the theology of the cross, see Douglas John Hall, *Lighten Our Darkness: Toward an Indigenous Theology of the Cross* (Philadelphia: Westminster, 1976).

4. Douglas John Hall, "The Theology of the Cross and Covenanting for Peace." Paper presented at a gathering of the World Council of Churches' Program for Justice, Peace and the Integrity of Creation, in Geneva, November 1986.

5. Charles Villa-Vicencio, "Right Wing Religion: Have the Chickens Come Home to Roost?," *Journal of Theology for Southern Africa*, December 1989, 7–16.

6. Ibid., 10–11.

7. Lincoln, *Race, Religion and the Continuing American Dilemma*, p. 31.

8. The Evangelical Lutheran Church in America, with churchwide offices in Chicago. As a result of a merger of several Lutheran churches, a new constitution was written, within which is written a multicultural vision for the church.

9. Lincoln, *Race, Religion and the Continuing American Dilemma*, 258, 260.

Chapter 7

1. Lincoln, *Race, Religion and the Continuing American Dilemma*, 259.

2. A speech by Jim Wallis at the convocation on Justice, Peace and the Integrity of Creation in Seoul, Korea, March 1990, quoted from *One World*, publication of the World Council of Churches, May 1990.

3. See bibliography for a partial listing of multicultural resources.

4. Bailey Jackson and Evangelina Hovino, "Developing Multicultural Organization," *Journal of Religion and Behavioral Sciences*, Fall 1988, 14.

5. Martin Luther King Jr., "Where Do We Go from Here: Chaos or Community?" 633.

6. The three primary kairos documents are *Challenge to the Churches: the Kairos Document* (from South Africa, 1985), *Kairos Central America: Challenge to the Churches of the World* (from Central America, 1988), and *The Road to Damascus: Kairos and Conversion* (from South Africa, Namibia, Nicaragua, Guatamala, El Salvador, South Korea, and the Philippines, 1989). These three documents have been published in one volume, *Kairos: Three Prophetic Challenges to the Church* (Grand Rapids: Eerdmans, 1991).

7. *The Kairos Convenant: Standing with South African Christians*, edited by Willis Logan (Oak Park, Ill.: Meyer-Stone Books; New York: Friendship Press, 1988), 7, 40.

8. *The Road to Damascus: Kairos and Conversion* (Washington, D.C.: Center of Concern Publishing, 1989), 26, 27.

SELECTED BIBLIOGRAPHY

Allen, Robert. *Reluctant Reformers: The Impact of Racism on American Social Movements.* Washington, D.C.: Howard University Press, 1974.

Allport, Gordon. *The Nature of Prejudice.* Reading, Mass.: Addison-Wesley Publishing Company, 1986.

America's Original Sin: A Study Guide on White Racism. Washington, D.C.: Sojourners Resource Center, 1988.

Anderson, Alan B., and George Pickering. *Confronting the Color Line: The Broken Promise of the Civil Rights Movement in Chicago.* Athens: The University of Georgia Press, 1986.

Bowser, Benjamin P., and Raymond Hunt, eds. *Impacts of Racism on White Americans.* Newbury Park, Calif.: Sage Publications, 1981.

Brown, Dee. *Bury My Heart at Wounded Knee: An Indian History of the American West.* New York: Holt, Rinehart & Winston, 1971.

Carmichael, Stokely, and Charles Hamilton. *Black Power: The Politics of Liberation in America.* New York: Vintage, 1967.

Cobbs, Price, and William Grier. *Black Rage.* New York: Basic Books, 1980.

Davis, Angela Yvonne. *Women, Race and Class.* New York: Vintage, 1983.

Davis, James H., and Woodie W. White. *Racial Transition in the Church.* Nashville: Abingdon, 1980.

Diamond, Sara. *Spiritual Warfare: The Politics of the Christian Right.* Boston: South End Press, 1989.

Du Bois, W. E. B. *Against Racism: Unpublished Essays and Papers, 1887–1961.* Edited by Herbert Aptheker. Amherst: University of Massachusetts Press, 1985.

Duchrow, Ulrich. *Global Economy: A Confessional Issue for the Churches?* Geneva: World Council of Churches, 1987.

"Eyes on the Prize: America's Civil Rights Years 1954–1965." Video history series. Boston: Blackside, Inc., 1987.

Farley, Reynolds. *Blacks and Whites: Narrowing the Gap?* Boston: Harvard University Press, 1984.

Fitzgerald, Kelly, ed. *Racism: The Church's Unfinished Agenda.* Washington, D.C.: United Methodist Church General Commission on Religion and Race, 1987.

Freire, Paulo. *Pedogogy of the Oppressed.* New York: Herder and Herder, 1972.

Gifford, Paul. *The Religious Right in Southern Africa.* Harare: University of Zimbabwe Publications, 1988.

Hate Groups in America: A Record of Bigotry and Violence. New York: Anti-Defamation League of B'nai B'rith, 1982.

Helms, Janet E., ed. *Black and White Racial Identity: Theory, Research and Practice.* New York: Greenwood Press, 1990.

Kairos: Three Prophetic Challenges to the Church. Grand Rapids: Eerdmans, 1991.

Katz, Judy H. *White Awareness: Handbook for Anti-Racism Training.* Norman: University of Oklahoma Press, 1978.

King, Martin Luther Jr. *A Testament of Hope: The Essential Writings of Martin Luther King, Jr.* Edited by James M. Washington. San Francisco: Harper and Row, 1986.

Kochman, Thomas. *Black and White Styles in Conflict.* Chicago: University of Chicago Press, 1981.

Knowles, Louis L., and Kenneth Prewitt. *Institutional Racism in America.* Englewood Cliffs, N.J.: Prentice-Hall, 1969.

Lincoln, C. Eric. *Race, Religion and the Continuing American Dilemma.* New York: Hill and Wang, 1984.

Lutz, Chris. *They Don't All Wear Sheets: A Chronology of Racist and Far Right Violence, 1980–1986.* Division of Church and Society of the National Council of Churches of Christ in the U.S.A. Atlanta: Center for Democratic Renewal, 1987.

Marable, Manning. *How Capitalism Underdeveloped Black America.* Boston: South End Press, 1983.

Matthias, Dody. *Working for Life: Dismantling Racism.* (A Book of Group Exercises.) Philadelphia: Huperetai, 1986.

McClain, William B. *Travelling Light.* New York: Friendship, 1981.

Myrdal, Gunnar. *An American Dilemma*. New York: Harper and Row, 1944.

Nelson-Pallmeyer, Jack. *War Against the Poor: Low Intensity Conflict and Christian Faith*. Maryknoll, N.Y.: Orbis, 1989.

Omi, Michael, and Howard Winant. *Racial Formation in the United States from the 1960s to the 1980s*. New York: Routledge and Kegan Paul, 1986.

Perlo, Victor. *Economics of Racism USA*. London: International Publishers, 1980.

Pero, Albert, and Ambrose Mayo. *Theology and the Black Experience*. Minneapolis: Augsburg, 1988.

Pettigrew, Thomas F. *Modern Racism: American Black-White Relations Since 1960s*. Cambridge: Harvard University Press, 1989.

Preiswerk, Roy, ed. *The Slant of the Pen: Racism in Children's Books*. Geneva: World Council of Churches, 1980.

Report of the National Advisory Commission on Civil Disorders (Kerner Report). New York: Bantam Books, 1968.

Rothenberg, Paula S. *Racism and Sexism: An Integrated Study*. New York: St. Martin's Press, 1988.

Schniedewind, Nancy, and Ellen Davidson. *Open Minds to Equality: A Sourcebook of Learning Activities to Promote Race, Sex, Class and Age Equality*. Englewood Cliffs, N.J.: Prentice-Hall, 1983.

Simms, Richard L., and Gloria Contreras, eds. *Racism and Sexism: Responding to the Challenge*. Washington, D.C.: National Council for the Social Studies, 1980.

Terry, Robert W. *For Whites Only*. Grand Rapids: Eerdmans, 1988.

Wilson, William Julius. *The Truly Disadvantaged: The Inner City, the Underclass, and Public Policy*. Chicago: University of Chicago Press, 1987.

Wright, Bruce. *Black Robes, White Justice*. New York: Lyle Stuart, 1987.